Pass Trinity now
GESE Grades 5-6
ISE I

Contents

	Page	Grammar	Functions
GRADE 5			
UNIT 1 Festivals & special occasions			
	8	The Present Perfect	Talking about the indefinite and recent past
UNIT 2 Means of transport			
	16	*Will* referring to the future Expressions of quantity	Informing & predicting about the future Quantifying
UNIT 3 Entertainment & music			
	24	Expressions of preference	Expressing preferences
UNIT 4 Recent personal experiences			
	32	Connecting clauses	Giving reasons Stating the duration of events
Review Units 1-2-3-4			40
GRADE 6			
UNIT 5 Fashion & money			
	42	Past Continuous	Describing past actions over a period of time
UNIT 6 Travel			
	50	Present Continuous for future use Infinitive of purpose	Expressing intention & purpose Expressing & requesting opinions
UNIT 7 Learning a language; Rules & regulations			
	58	Modals for obligation, necessity and uncertainty	Expressing obligation, necessity & uncertainty
UNIT 8 Health & fitness			
	66	Zero and first conditional	Expressing surprise
Review units 5-6-7-8			74

Contents

Phonology	Exam Expert Topic (T) & Conversation (C)	Writing
Have in the Present Perfect	Preparing for the Topic phase (T) Dos and don'ts (C)	Exam practice
Intonation of basic question forms	Preparing & discussing your topic (T)	Exam practice
Intonation of more complex question forms	Responding to the examiner (T) Exam practice (C)	Exam practice
-ed past tense endings	Showing understanding of the examiner (C) Exam practice (C)	Exam practice
Sentence stress to clarify meaning	Preparing questions for the interview (C)	Exam practice
–	Exam practice (C) Topic structure (T) Dos and don'ts (T)	Exam practice
Connected speech at sentence level	Talking about rules and regulation (C)	Exampractice
Intonation at sentence level and of more complex forms	Exam practice (C) Choosing a topic (T)	Exam practice

Trinity Grades 5-6 Overview	4	ISE file	78
Diagnostic test	6	Appendix: Extra material	95
Trinity Takeaway	76		

3

Exam overview

TRINITY GRADED EXAMINATIONS IN SPOKEN ENGLISH (GESE), GRADES 5 AND 6, AND INTEGRATED SKILLS IN ENGLISH (ISE), LEVEL I

GESE Grades 5 & 6 (CEFR B1)

Time: 10 minutes

Format and procedure:

1 Discussion of a **topic prepared by the candidate** (up to 5 minutes):
- Give **information about the prepared topic** and **answer questions**.
- **Ask the examiner at least one question** about the topic area.

2 Conversation on two subject areas selected by the examiner (up to 5 minutes):
- **Answer appropriately** to questions and give information **in simple and direct exchanges**.
- **Ask the examiner at least one question** (Grade 5)/**two questions** (Grade 6) about the subject areas.

Grade 5 exam syllabus:

Grammar
- Present Perfect tense including use with *for, since, ever, never, just*
- connecting clauses using *because*
- *will* for informing and predicting the future
- adjectives and adverbials of quantity, e.g. *a lot (of), not very much, many...*
- expressions of preference, e.g. *I prefer, I'd rather...*

Subject areas for Conversation phase
- festivals
- means of transport
- special occasions, e.g. birthday celebrations
- entertainment, e.g. cinema, television, clubs
- music
- recent personal experiences

Functions
- talking about the future (informing and predicting)
- expressing preferences
- talking about events in the indefinite and recent past
- giving reasons
- stating the duration of events
- quantifying

Phonology
- correct pronunciation of words relevant to the vocabulary for this grade
- combination of weak forms and contractions, e.g. *I've been to...*
- avoidance of speech patterns of recitation

Exam overview

Grade 6 exam syllabus:

Grammar
- zero and first conditionals, using *if* and *when*
- Present Continuous tense for future use
- Past Continuous tense
- modals: *must*, *need to*, *might*, *don't have to*
- infinitive of purpose

Subject areas for Conversation phase
- travel
- money
- fashion
- rules and regulations
- health and fitness
- learning a foreign language

Functions
- expressing and requesting opinions and impressions
- expressing intention and purpose
- expressing obligation and necessity
- expressing certainty and uncertainty
- describing past actions over a period of time

Phonology
- correct pronunciation of words relevant to the vocabulary for this grade
- sentence stress to clarify meaning
- intonation patterns of more complex question forms
- basic intonation of connected speech
- avoidance of speech patterns of recitation

ISE I

Speaking and Listening
Format: a speaking exam with two tasks and a listening exam with two tasks
Time: 14 minutes

Speaking
- **Discussion** of a **topic** prepared by the candidate (up to 4 minutes)
- **Conversation** with the examiner about **one subject area** from Grade 6 list selected by the examiner (2 minutes).

Independent Listening
- **Task 1**: candidates **listen** to a **description** or a **narrative** and **respond to questions** asked by the examiner (3 minutes, 15 seconds).
- **Task 2**: candidates **listen** to a **factual text**, **report information** from it to the examiner and **respond to questions** asked by the examiner (3 minutes, 45 seconds).

Reading and writing
Format: a reading and writing exam with four tasks
Time: 2 hours

Procedure
- **Task 1, Long reading**: candidates **read one long text** of approximately 400 words and answer 15 questions (20 minutes).
- **Task 2, Multi-text reading**: candidates **read four texts** of different types related to the same topic and totalling approximately 400 words and **answer 15 questions** (20 minutes).
- **Task 3, Reading into writing**: candidates **write a text** of 100-130 words in response to a prompt, **using information from the four texts in Task 2** (40 minutes).
- **Task 4, Extended writing**: candidates **write a text** of 100-130 words in response to a prompt (40 minutes).

Diagnostic test

 Listen to the examiner asking some questions and choose the best answer, A, B or C. There is only one right answer for each question. You will hear each question only ONCE. Good luck!

1
A My name Gianluca.
B My name's Gianluca.
C Is Gianluca.

2
A I've 17.
B I'm 17.
C Fine, thanks. And You?

3
A She's blue.
B He's blue.
C It's blue.

4
A There are seven.
B They are seven.
C We have seven.

5
A I am of Trieste.
B I come to Trieste.
C I come from Trieste.

6
A Yes, I got a dog.
B Yes, I've got a dog.
C Yes, I have got.

7
A Her name is Paola.
B She name is Paola.
C Her name Paola.

8
A He has two.
B He is two.
C He two.

9
A It's opposite of the supermarket.
B It opposite the supermarket.
C It's opposite the supermarket.

10
A It's today.
B It's Monday.
C Is Monday.

11
A I live in Madrid.
B I live at Madrid.
C I live to Madrid.

12
A It's raining.
B It rains.
C It was cloudy.

13
A It rained.
B It rains.
C It was rain.

14
A the third of March
B the three of March
C three March

15
A Yes, I do.
B Yes, I can.
C Yes, I have.

16
A in 7 o'clock
B on 7 o'clock
C at 7 o'clock

17
A I'm watching TV.
B I watched TV.
C I watch TV.

18
A They are drinking coffee.
B They are drink coffee.
C They drink coffee.

Diagnostic test

19
A Yes, of course.
B Yes, I help you.
C Yes, I do.

20
A No, I didn't.
B No, I don't.
C No, I haven't.

21
A No, I didn't go for holiday.
B Yes, I went to the beach.
C No, I haven't.

22
A I enjoy swimming.
B I enjoy to swim.
C I enjoy to swimming.

23
A I was watching television.
B I watch television.
C I watched television.

24
A Sarah is the better student.
B Sarah is best student.
C Sarah is the best student.

25
A London is bigger.
B London is more bigger.
C London is more big.

26
A I have bought them last weekend.
B I buy them last weekend.
C I bought them last weekend.

27
A twice a week
B twice in the week
C two times the week

28
A I will visiting my Aunt.
B I'm going for visit my Aunt.
C I'm going to visit my Aunt.

29
A Yes, once a week.
B Yes, sometimes a week.
C Yes, one time a week.

30
A Yes, I went to Edinburgh last year.
B Yes, I was in Cambridge.
C Yes, I have gone to London.

31
A Because I want to have a certificate.
B Because of a certificate.
C Because to have a certificate.

32
A at about midday
B I've had lunch.
C Yes, I have had lunch.

33
A Yes, there is much.
B Yes, there is many.
C Yes, there is a lot.

34
A I was here since two years.
B I've been here since two years.
C I've been here for two years.

35
A I am prefer dance music.
B I am preferring dance music.
C I prefer dance music.

36
A I'm preferring to travel by car.
B I prefer to travel by a car.
C I prefer to travel by car.

37
A I think to go for a coffee.
B I think I will to go for a coffee.
C I think I'll go for a coffee.

38
A No, I've never had any.
B No, I didn't.
C No, I never tasted it.

39
A since I was 12
B for long time
C since 5 years

40
A two days before
B two days ago
C two days early

UNIT 1
Festivals & special occasions

GRADE 5

A 4
B 1
C 6
D 3
E 8
F 2
G 7
H 5

Vocabulary

1a Match the photos (A-H) with the festivals and special occasions (1-8).

1 Christmas
2 Valentine's Day
3 a graduation
4 a wedding
5 Halloween
6 New Year
7 Carnival
8 a birthday

b Think of all the other festivals and special occasions you can. Write them, and the ones in the pictures above, in the table.

British	national	international

Festivals & special occasions

2a In pairs, match the words from the box with each celebration. You may decide to put some words in more than one picture. Use a dictionary if you need to.

> rings   carols   bride & groom   pumpkin
> lovers   fireworks   chocolates   ghosts   cards
> witches   decorations   resolutions   presents
> Boxing Day   midnight   the best man   roses

b Now use the definitions of seven words from a) to complete the crossword.

> midnight   pumpkin   cards   chocolates
> decorations   roses   fireworks

Across

1 On New Year's Eve we stay up until this time.
3 We send these to friends and family at Christmas and on birthdays.
5 They are loud and colourful and we use them to celebrate special occasions.
6 They are sweet and we often eat them on special occasions, like Christmas.
7 This orange vegetable is popular at Halloween.

Down

2 People often put these up around the house at Christmas.
4 People give these flowers to say, 'I love you'.

c 🔊 Listen to the four speakers. Which festival is each person describing?

3 Work in small groups, and choose a festival from this unit or another one from your country or region. Then follow these instructions.

1 List the things that people do and eat at this festival.
2 Expand the information by making notes about the items on your list.
3 Now one person from the group presents the festival to the rest of the class, without saying the name of the festival.
4 The rest of the class tries to name the festival.

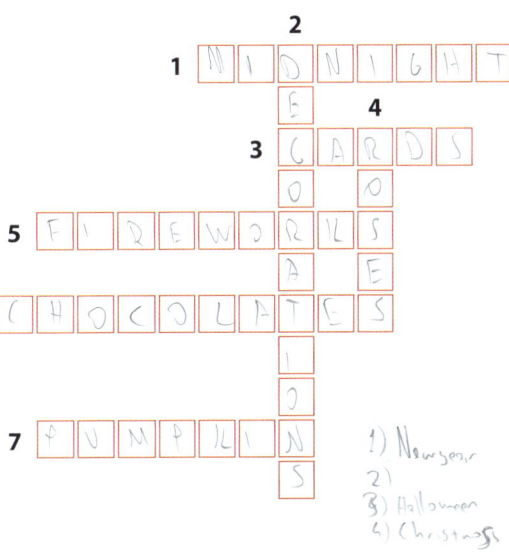

UNIT 1

Grammar focus

The Present Perfect

The Present Perfect is formed with *have/has* + the past participle (verb + *-ed*).
e.g. She **has eaten** too much cake.

In English, there are two main ways to talk about the past:
1 We use the **Past Simple** to talk about experiences with a **specific reference** to when the event happened. We use time expressions such as *yesterday, last week/month/year, in 1999, in January*.
I **went** to Venice in 2006.

2 We use the **Present Perfect** to talk about experiences when there is **no reference** to when the event happened. We use *for, since, ever, never* and *just*.
I've **been** to Venice twice.
They've **celebrated** Carnival **for** hundreds of years.
She's **lived** in Hong Kong **since** 1998.
They've **never spent** New Year's Eve in Scotland.
They've **just come back** from holiday. (They were on holiday last week.)
Have you **ever received** a Valentine's Day card?

4 Look at the sentences below and decide whether they contain the Present Perfect (A) or Past Simple (B).

0 B   I went to Edinburgh last year.
1 ☐   Jenny phoned Susan last night.
2 ☐   She has told us all the details.
3 ☐   Have you ever played basketball?
4 ☐   Brian has received a letter from Lia.
5 ☐   They opened their presents around the tree.
6 ☐   Emilio has never been to Venice.

5a Look at these rules for using *for, since, ever, never* and *just* with the Present Perfect in English and complete them by putting the right word into each space. (Use the examples above to help you).

We use…
1 …………… when we want to focus on a period of time.
2 …………… when we want to focus on the date or the time when a period began.
3 …………… to emphasise that something has happened very recently.
4 …………… when something has not happened at any time in the past.
5 …………… when we want to ask questions about experiences in the past.

Festivals & special occasions

b Complete the following sentences using *for*, *since*, *ever*, *never* or *just*.

1. Have you .... seen a film starring Brad Pitt?
2. They've been in the football team .... last year.
3. I haven't seen Bruno .... ages!
4. She has .... moved to Madrid – her dad got a new job last month.
5. I've .... been to a film festival!
6. Have you .... been to a wedding?

c Go around the class asking questions beginning with *Have you ever...?* Try to find people who have done each of the activities in the list below.

Find someone who...

1. has eaten raw fish.   ....
2. has been to Greece.   ....
3. has been to an eighteenth birthday celebration.   ....
4. has seen a James Bond film.   ....
5. has been skiing.   ....
6. has played a musical instrument in public.   ....

d Now choose two of the activities above and ask more questions to find more information (use the box below to help you).

Remember!

We often begin conversations using the **Present Perfect** to ask about experiences. Then we may change to the **Past Simple** to continue talking about details of the experience.

A: *Have you ever been to London?*
B: *Yes, I have. In fact I've just been there.*
A: *When did you go there?*
B: *I went there last month.*
A: *Did you visit the Tower of London?*
B: *No, I didn't have time!*

Phonology

6a 🔊 Listen to these sentences with *have* in the Present Perfect. Do we use contractions in the positive, negative and interrogative forms?

1. I**'ve** been to Venice.
2. I **haven't** been to Venice.
3. **Have** you been to Venice? Yes, I **have**./No, I **haven't**.

b Practice saying these sentences with a partner.

1. They've finished their studies.
2. He's been to Paris.
3. Peter's gone shopping.
4. Yes, she has.
5. No, she hasn't.
6. Have you ever eaten roast beef?
7. I've been in the queue for hours!
8. She's just finished her shower.

c 🔊 Now listen to the sentences and repeat them.

UNIT 1

Reading

7a Read this article about a festival and find out where it is.

b Say what these numbers from the text refer to.

1 825
2 three
3 six
4 1591
5 200

c Underline all the expressions that you can find in the article which refer to the past. Which tense is used? Why?

d Without looking at the text, work with a partner and tell them about the Bull Run in Pamplona. Use the following words in your sentences.

1 Pamplona bull run/happen/nearly every year since 1591
2 recent years/become/big tourist attraction
3 fire/rocket/confirm/gate/just open
4 you/ever/see/spectacle/this?

Writing

ISE → See ISE file on page 92

8 Imagine that you went to the Pamplona Bull Run with some friends. Write a review (100-130 words) of your experience for a travel website. You should:

- describe what you saw
- explain what you preferred about the festival
- say if you will go to the festival again.

THE BULL RUN

The bull run in Pamplona, northern Spain, has happened nearly every year since 1591. In recent years it has become a big tourist attraction. It takes place at 8 a.m. every morning from 7th to 14th July. Runners must be ready by 7.30 a.m. The actual run goes from the corral at Santo Domingo where the bulls are kept, to the bullring where they fight that same afternoon. The length of the run is 825 metres and the average time of the run from start to finish is about three minutes. The streets through the old town which make up the bull run are closed off, so the bulls can't escape. Each day six fighting bulls run the route.

The tension builds as the release of the bulls approaches and at 8 a.m. on the dot they fire a rocket to confirm that the gate has just opened at the Santo Domingo corral. The runners, who are dressed in white with a red handkerchief around their necks, pray to San Fermín. Then a second rocket announces that the bulls have left. The bulls and the runners then run along the route. Sometimes people get hurt.

Have you ever seen a spectacle like this? No? Then start planning your trip!

exam EXPERT

Topic phase
■ Preparing for the Topic phase

The Topic phase is the first part of the exam. You must prepare a topic before the exam to discuss with the examiner. This topic must **not** be from the list of subject areas from the Trinity exam specifications.

9 Complete this information about the Topic phase with the verbs in the box.

> prepare   learn   interests   remember   add

Choosing my topic

Choose a topic that ¹.................. you so that it is easy to speak about it. Make sure that you know, or can ².................., enough grammar and vocabulary to be able to speak about it.

Preparing my topic

You must prepare a mind map with five discussion points on it. This will help you to ³.................. what you want to say. You can also take one or two photos or objects into the exam to illustrate your topic.
Do not memorise your topic! If the examiner thinks you have memorised it, she or he will automatically interrupt you.

Length of topic

The topic section of the exam is no more than 5 minutes. ⁴.................. some ideas on your topic, as you will have a discussion about it with the examiner.

How to create a mind map

- Write the title of the topic in the middle of a piece of paper.
- ⁵.................. five ideas about the topic around the title.
- Then think of 3 or 4 sentences for each idea.
- Make sure you are using Grade 5 language as much as possible in your sentences.
- At least one of your sentences must be a question that you ask the examiner.

10a Peter is an English teacher in Mexico. He is going to speak about Christmas in Britain with his friend, José, to give his class an example of the topic. Before you listen to Peter's topic, put a tick in column A against the ideas you think he will include in his discussion.

		A	B
2	Special food	☐	☐
2	Christmas carols	☐	☐
3	Christmas cards	☐	☐
4	Presents	☐	☐
5	Watching TV	☐	☐
6	Playing games	☐	☐

b 🔊 Now listen to Peter's topic and tick (✓) the ideas he talks about in column B.

13

exam EXPERT

c 🔊 In the topic you will need to use Grade 5 language, like using the present perfect, expressing preferences, giving reasons, using a *lot/much/many* and expressing the future. You will also need to use language from the lower Grades, for example, the present tense, the past tense, *going to* and *like doing*. Listen to Peter's conversation again and as you listen tick the language items you hear.

1. ☐ because
2. ☐ a lot of
3. ☐ many
4. ☐ present simple 'we buy'
5. ☐ prefer
6. ☐ love/like doing
7. ☐ simple past 'came'
8. ☐ going to future
9. ☐ will future

d Listen again and answer the questions.
1. Why does Peter like Christmas so much?
2. What does Peter do before Christmas?
3. What does Peter prefer doing at Christmas?
4. What does he like doing with his nephews and nieces?
5. Why was last Christmas special? How does he describe it?
6. What's he going to do next Christmas?

e Look at Peter's mind map for his topic. In pairs see if you can remember what Peter said about each point. Then make a mind map about a festival you have celebrated.

Conversation

Dos and don'ts

11 Complete the advice about the conversation phase by writing *Do* or *Don't* to start each sentence.

0. *Do* answer the question you are asked!
00. *Don't* just answer yes or no when the examiner asks you a question!
1. .... start an answer with *Let me think...*, or *Let's see...*, if you need extra time.
2. .... pause for too long before answering.
3. .... be prepared to give reasons for, or more details about, something you say.
4. .... remember that it's alright to talk about something ordinary – not having done something really exciting isn't an excuse for not talking!
5. .... ask the examiner at least one question in Grade 5, at least two in Grade 6 and for ISE I. You could ask about the subject she/he has just asked you about.
6. .... show interest in and/or comment on the answer the examiner gives to your question/s, with expressions such as, *That sounds nice.*, *That sounds like fun.*, *How nice! Really?*

Mind map: **CHRISTMAS IN BRITAIN**
- 1 Preparations for Christmas
- 2 Christmas Day
- 3 Why I like Christmas
- 4 The best Christmas ever
- 5 What I prefer about Christmas

Listening to Peter speaking about Christmas will help you in both the Topic and Conversation phase, but remember, in the actual exam, you will have to choose a topic that is not on the list of Subject areas for the conversation, so you will need to choose something different to talk about.

exam EXPERT

Writing

12 Put the different stages (A-H) of doing a writing task into the correct order.

- A ☐ Write a first draft.
- B ☐ Listen to what your partner says about how you can improve your text.
- C ☐ Write a plan for your text.
- D ☐ Write a second draft.
- E ☐ Give your text to your teacher.
- F ☐ Swap texts with a partner and suggest ways for your partner to improve her/his text.
- G ☐ Refer to exercises in this unit for help with subject area vocabulary and grammar.
- H ☐ Refer to the Writing file for help with how to write the text type.

ISE → See ISE file on pages 90 and 92

13 Choose one, of these writing tasks and follow the stages in Exercise 12.

An email

It is a friend's 18th birthday soon. You and a group of friends want to buy him/her a special present. Write an email (100-130 words) to your group of friends. You should:
- explain what will be a suitable present for your friend
- say how your friend is planning to celebrate his/her birthday.

A review

You recently went to a music festival. Write a review (100-130 words) for a music magazine. You should:
- describe the different types of music at the festival
- say if you will go to another music festival in the future.

Examiner: Is there a special festival in your town?
Candidate: Yes, we celebrate St Stephen's Day – he's the Saint of our local church. We parade through the streets and we have special St Stephen's cakes – they are really delicious. Have you tried one?

15

UNIT 2
Means of transport

A ....

B ....

C ....

D ....

E ....

F ....

Vocabulary

1a Label the pictures with a word from the box below.

> car helicopter train port minibus
> runway tram bicycle cruise ship bus
> coach underground airport taxi
> lighthouse ferry terminal

b Put the words from the box into the appropriate column of the table (some can go in more than one column). Use a dictionary to help you if you need to.

Air	
Sea	
Land	

Means of transport

Phonology
Intonation of basic question forms

2a 🔊 Listen to these two examples and notice the difference in the intonation.

1 What's your name? (▼)
2 Do you speak any other languages? (▲)

b 🔊 Now listen to these questions. Write them and decide if the end of the question goes up (▲) or down (▼).

1 ....
2 ....
3 ....
4 ....
5 ....
6 ....

🔊 Listen to the questions again and repeat them using the same intonation.

Vocabulary
Transport survey

3a You are going to take part in a class survey on transport and travel. With a partner, practise asking and answering the questions below.

Questions about transport

| How do you | usually normally | come get | to | school? university? class? |

Answers about transport

I come	on	foot
		my bike/bicycle/motorbike/scooter
	by	car/bus/train/bike

| I | take catch get | a the | bus/train/tram/underground |

| I get a lift | from with | my mother a friend |

Questions about travel time

| How long | does it take (you) do you take | to get to come | to | school? class? |

Answers about travel time

It takes about half an hour.
It takes an hour if I'm lucky!
It depends on the traffic!

UNIT 2

b Now work in groups and ask everyone in your group questions about how they travel every day. Note their answers on the survey record sheet below.

c When you have collected all your results and calculated the totals answer the following questions about your group.

1. What is the most popular form of transport?
2. What is the least popular form of transport?
3. Who has the quickest and who has the longest journey?
4. How many people travel by car? How many people travel by bike?

In your answers to these questions try to use expressions such as, *all of us, most of us, a lot of us, not very many of us* and *none of us*.

Reading

4a Read the explanation of 'no-frills' and conventional airlines. Then work with a partner. Ask and answer the questions below.

When you buy an airline ticket you are really paying simply to travel from one place to another. Conventional airlines usually give you a drink, a meal, a magazine or a newspaper to read. These are 'frills' – in other words, extra services. '**No-frills**' airlines often offer cheap tickets, but no extra services.

1. Have you ever travelled with a 'no-frills' airline?
2. If so, what was the journey like?
3. Would you recommend that airline to a friend?

b Read the text about 'no-frills' airlines and put the three headings below in the right place in the text. Decide which type of airline you prefer and talk to a partner about your reasons.

1. What won't you get?
2. What will you get with both 'no-frills' and conventional airlines?
3. What will you get with a 'no-frills' airline?

Name	....	....	....	....	....
walk					
bus					
tram					
underground					
train					
taxi					
lift					
drive a car					
motorbike					
bicycle					
journey time in minutes					
Total					

Means of transport

'NO-FRILLS' AIRLINES

In recent years there has been a revolution in the travel industry. The conventional airlines now face strong competition from a new generation of progressive airlines, so-called 'low-cost'. With their low **fares** and simple procedures these airlines are both taking business away from the conventional airlines and creating a new travel market of people who are encouraged to travel simply because low fares are available.

A ....
Well, you will get taken from one airport to another. You may not fly to the airports you would normally choose. They will probably be small and some way from the city they actually serve. You will also get a low, or in some cases, a very low, fare. You may find that people rush forward at the **boarding gate** to get their favourite seats on the plane.

B ....
Normally you won't get a choice of class – business or first class aren't usually available. You probably won't have a ticket. You will probably not be able **to book** your flight through a **travel agent**. You won't get any free snacks, drinks or meals. You probably won't get a choice between an a window and an **aisle seat**. You probably won't get an in-flight magazine or in-flight entertainment.

C ....
You will probably get a long **queue** at the **check-in desk**. You will run the risk of delays and losing your luggage!

c Match these definitions to the words or phrases highlighted in the text.

0 the place in the terminal where your ticket is checked   *check-in desk*
1 the place where you wait before you get on the plane   ....
2 another word for 'to reserve' a ticket   ....
3 the seat furthest from the window and closest to the centre   ....
4 a line of people   ....
5 the money that you pay in order to travel   ....
6 a person who organises travel and holidays   ....

d Look at the text again and then in pairs or small groups list the advantages and disadvantages of travel with a 'no-frills' airline.

Advantages	Disadvantages
cheap	airports may be far from city centres

Writing

ISE ➡ See ISE file on pages 87 and 88

5 Your school is planning an end-of-term trip to London for your class. Your teacher has asked you to find out about different ways of flying to the UK. Write an essay (100-130 words) for your teacher. You should:

- describe the different ways you can fly to London
- explain which one will be better for your trip.

UNIT 2

Will referring to the future

Forming the future with will
The future with *will* is formed by adding *will* to the base form of the verb (infinitive without *to*).
I + will + go   I + will not (won't) + go

In speech and informal writing we normally contract the subject with *will*.
I will → I'll   you will → you'll   we will → we'll

Using will for the future
Will has many different meanings for future reference.
Two of these are predicting and informing about the future.

1 Predicting
I think I'**ll finish** my degree next year.
I'**ll probably be** a lawyer when I finish my studies.

2 Informing
The journey to Brighton **will take** two hours.
We **won't be able to** buy tickets on the bus.

We often use *will* to make predictions with words like *probably* and after verbs which indicate a decision or judgement.
I'**ll probably take** the train to work tomorrow.
I **think I'll take** a holiday next week.
I'm **sure you'll be** here in time for dinner.
I **imagine they'll win** easily.

6a Here are some questions about the future with possible answers. Try to match the questions (1-5) with the right answers (A-F).

0   [A]   What do you plan to do after your studies?
1   [ ]   What are Emilio's plans for university?
2   [ ]   What do you hope to do this weekend?
3   [ ]   What job does Emilio **not** want to do?
4   [ ]   What will you do if there's nothing on TV tonight?
5   [ ]   Is there a particular programme you want to see?

A I'll probably become a teacher.
B He won't be a bus driver!
C He'll probably study town planning.
D In that case I'll read or go to bed early.
E Yes, the football – I'm sure we'll win!
F I'll probably go to the cinema.

b Complete the tour guide's information using a *will* future for informing and the verbs below.

include   take   leave   be

'Good morning everyone. We would like to inform you of one or two changes to our programme for tomorrow. The bus tour of the city centre ¹.............. the hotel at 9.45, but don't worry, you ².............. back at the hotel in time for dinner at 6 p.m. The tour ³.............. about five hours and ⁴.............. a stop for lunch in the old part of the city. We hope you have a pleasant trip!'

c Think about transport in your town/city. What do you think will be the major problems in the next decade? Complete the sentences below with your ideas.

1 I think...   3 I imagine...
2 I'm sure...   4 ...will probably...

Now exchange ideas with the person next to you. Do you agree or disagree?

exam EXPERT

Topic phase
■ **Preparing and discussing your topic**

7a Look at this photo of Turin. What types of transport can you see? Compare it with your own city or home town. What is different? What is the same? Talk about this with a partner.

b 🔊 Emilio is a Grade 5 candidate from Turin. Emilio wants to get some speaking practice and is going to discuss a topic with his teacher. He has made up a topic form to practise speaking about 'Transport in Turin'. For the exam Emilio is going to choose another subject of interest to him, which is not on the subject list for Grade 5. Listen to the recording and number the points on the form in the order in which you hear Emilio talking about them.

c 🔊 Listen again and decide whether these statements are true (T) or false (F).

1. ☐ Emilio prefers using the tram.
2. ☐ Emilio has just moved to Turin.
3. ☐ Turin has an underground railway.

4. ☐ Turin's transport control system has made journeys quicker.
5. ☐ Emilio won't be a bus driver in the future.

d Now talk to a partner and decide whether you would like to visit Turin. Is it like your home town?

☐ The transport I prefer

☐ My Dad's job in transport

☐ My future job in transport

Transport in Turin

☐ Turin, my home town

☐ Future transport in Turin

exam EXPERT

8a Emilio made extra mind maps to help him prepare his topic. Each mind map gives information about the main discussion points on his Topic form. Look at the extra information about Turin below.

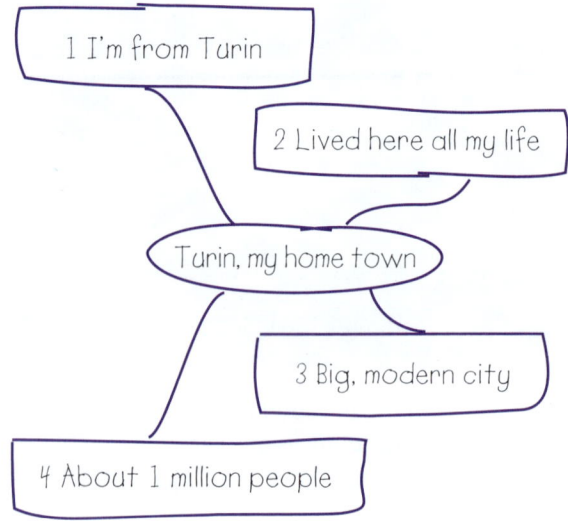

- 1 I'm from Turin
- 2 Lived here all my life
- Turin, my home town
- 3 Big, modern city
- 4 About 1 million people

The transport I prefer — 1 .... 2 .... 3 ....

My dad's job in transport — 4 .... 5 .... 6 ....

Future transport in Turin — 7 .... 8 .... 9 .... 10 ....

My future job in transport — 11 ....

b 🔊 Listen to Emilio's discussion again and as you listen, complete the extra mind maps below to give more information about the other discussion points.

c 🔊 Remember! Don't memorise your topic. Listen to the same topic discussion, but this time the candidate has memorised it. What differences are there between the two versions? What do you notice about the candidate's intonation?

You have listened to Emilio talking about Transport to practice speaking about the subject area of Transport. For the exam you need to choose a subject for your own Topic that is not one of the subject areas for GESE 5. In the exam you will only have the five main points on your mind map – you won't be able to use notes.

exam EXPERT

9 Complete these sentences about the Topic phase with *do* and *don't*.

Topic 'Do's and Don'ts'

1 .... memorise your topic! It may make you feel more confident but it will almost certainly spoil your pronunciation. In any case, the examiner will interrupt you!

2 .... practise using your mind map to remind you of what you planned to say.

3 .... link the points you are making together.

E.g. 'I come from Turin *and* I've lived here all my life. It's a big, modern city *with* a population of about a million people.'

4 .... remember – you must ask the examiner at least one question.

E.g. 'Have you ever been to Turin?'

5 .... be surprised if the examiner asks you to talk about your topic in a different order than you've put on your mind map.

Writing

ISE → *See ISE file on pages 89 and 90*

10 Choose one of these writing tasks.

An informal letter

Write a letter (100-130-words) to a friend. You should:

- say what you have to do to keep your bike in good condition
- explain why you enjoy riding it.

An article

Write an article (100-130 words) for a travel guide about the different ways of travelling around your country. You should:

- describe the different methods of transport
- explain how you prefer to travel.

Examiner: How do you normally travel to your classes?
Candidate: Well, it depends on the weather. It only takes me 20 minutes to walk to school, but if it's raining, my mother gives me a lift.

UNIT 3
Entertainment & music

GRADE 5

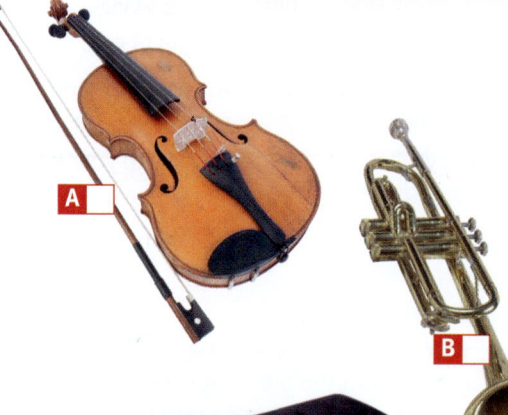

Vocabulary
Music

1a Match these instruments (1-10) to the pictures (A-J).

1	accordion	6	trumpet
2	keyboard	7	trombone
3	violin	8	drums
4	piano	9	guitar
5	organ	10	saxophone

b Do you know the names for the people who play these instruments? Put them in the right columns below.

-ist	-er	- player
accordionist	trumpeter	keyboard-player

TeachingEnglish

Text C

The Hong Kong Bun Festival

1. Find the meaning of the following words: pirate, drive away, bun, tower

2. Then read the text and fill in the table below.

This festival is held on the island on Cheung Chau in Hong Kong in early May every year, around the time of Buddha's birthday. The festival celebrates the god Pak Tai, who drove pirates and illness away from the island. In the festival, the islanders pray for safety from pirates and illness. The festival lasts for seven days. For three of those days everyone on the island is vegetarian. There is a procession through the village with lion dances, dragon dances and musicians. In the procession children in colourful costumes are carried high above people's heads. The islanders make three 20-metre high bamboo towers and cover these with buns. At midnight on the last day people light fires and then climb the towers to get the buns. They wear bags on their backs to collect the buns and when they come down from the towers, they give them to everyone who is watching. Then everyone celebrates with fireworks

Entertainment & music

c Work with a partner and take turns to ask and answer these questions.

1. Can you play a musical instrument? If so, which one?
2. Does any of your family or friends play an instrument?
3. Which instrument do you like listening to?
4. Do you prefer playing music or listening to music?

d Work with a partner and talk about music using the following example to help you.

A: Do you play a musical instrument?
B: No, I don't but my *sister's/father's/cousin's a guitarist/pianist/keyboard player/violinist*. And how about you? Do you play an instrument?

Or

B: Yes, I do. I play the piano. And how about you? Do you play an instrument?
A: No, I don't – I haven't got the patience to practise!

2a Do you know all these different types of music? Match the type with the musician.

1. ☐ hip hop   A Beethoven
2. ☐ rap   B Lady Gaga
3. ☐ classical   C Linkin Park
4. ☐ pop   D Shakira
5. ☐ folk   E Eminem
6. ☐ new metal   F Bob Marley
7. ☐ reggae   G Bob Dylan
8. ☐ dance   H The Black Eyed Peas

b Now talk about music with your partner. Ask and answer the following questions.

1. What kind of music do you like?
2. Do you ever listen to any of the musicians in a)?
3. When do you usually listen to music?
4. Have you ever been to a live concert or a music festival?

GRADE 5

UNIT 3

Film

3a How well do you know British films? Work in pairs and see how many answers you know to this quiz – if you don't know an answer, guess!

b Now work with another pair. Did you get the same answers? If not, decide which are the correct answers. Then, go to page 95 and check your answers.

c Look at these adjectives to describe films, books and TV programmes. Decide whether they are used to say you like the entertainment or you don't.

> boring dull exciting entertaining
> predictable moving funny fascinating
> beautiful slow silly interesting
> romantic great awful

Did you like the film?

No, it was really...   *Yes, it was really...*

d Now work in pairs. Use the adjectives from c) to describe a TV programme or a film you have seen recently.

Lights, Camera, Action! – a film quiz

1 The stars of *Notting Hill* were
   A Hugh Grant & Gwyneth Paltrow.   **B** Hugh Grant & Julia Roberts.   **C** Brad Pitt & Julia Roberts.

2 In the Harry Potter films, Harry's best friend is called
   A Hermione.   **B** Geraldine.   **C** Voldemort.

3 Renee Zellwegger starred in a film called *Bridget Jones's*
   A *Journal*.   **B** *Diary*.   **C** *Confessions*.

4 *Slumdog Millionaire* took place in
   A Scotland.   **B** The United States.   **C** India.

5 *Billy Elliot* was a film about
   A football.   **B** a famous jazz singer.
   C a boy who wants to be a ballet dancer.

6 In *Bend It Like Beckham*, the protagonist wants to become
   A a singer.   **B** a footballer.   **C** an actress.

7 *Sherlock Holmes* was directed by
   A David Lynch.   **B** Martin Scorsese.   **C** Guy Ritchie.

8 How many Oscars did *Shakespeare in Love* win?
   A 7   **B** 3   **C** 1

Entertainment & music

Grammar focus

Expressing preferences

There are several ways of talking about preferences in English. Here are two of them.

1 Talking about your preferences in general.
prefer + object + *to* + object
She **prefers** original versions **to** films with subtitles.

subject + *prefer* + + verb + *-ing* + *to* + verb + *-ing*
I **prefer** swimming **to** running

In conversation, the questions which would produce answers like these would be:

Which actor do you prefer – Gwyneth Paltrow or Julia Roberts?
What does she prefer – playing music or listening to it?

2 Talking about preferences on a specific occasion.
+ *would* ('d) *rather* + infinitive without *to* + *than* + infinitive without *to*
I**'d rather** go to Salsa classes **than** go to the gym.
He**'d rather** see Sherlock Holmes again **than** watch a romantic film.

In conversation, the questions which would produce answers like these would be:

What would you rather do – buy the CD or go to the concert?
What would you rather do – read a book or see a film?

4a Use the promts to make sentences using *prefer*.

0 I/Pierce Brosnan/Brad Pitt
   I prefer Pierce Brosnan to Brad Pitt
1 Giuseppe/play/music/listen/to it
2 She/Scarlett Johansson/Halle Berry
3 We/action films/romantic films
4 My mother/romantic novels/science fiction
5 They/go/cinema/watch DVDs

b Work in pairs. Ask and answer questions using the prompts below.

1 What/prefer/classical concerts/rock concerts?
2 Who/prefer/Robert Pattinson/Daniel Radcliffe?
3 What/prefer/visting/art galleries/museums?
4 Who/prefer/Rihanna/Lilly Allen?

c Now, think of three questions like these about entertainment to ask your partner, using the structures above.

5a Use the promts to make sentences using *rather*.

0 I/buy/CD/go/concert
   I'd rather buy a CD than go to a concert
1 They/read/book/see/film
2 He/meet/friends/do/homework
3 I/play football/watch it
4 My father/stay/home/go/party
5 She/travel for a year/go straight to University

UNIT 3

b Work in pairs. Ask and answer questions, using the prompts below.

1. What/rather/go/classical concert/rock concert?
2. What/rather/watch TV/listen/music?
3. What/rather/see/film/go/restaurant?
4. What/rather/go/walk/watch/DVD?

c Now, think of three questions like these about entertainment to ask your partner.

Phonology

Intonation of more complex question forms

6a Listen to these three questions asking about preferences. The arrows below show the direction of the speaker's voice.

1. Would you like tea or coffee?
2. Do you prefer Rihanna or Lilly Allen?
3. Would you rather go to the cinema or the theatre?

b Now listen to the questions again and repeat them using the same intonation.

c In pairs, write questions using the prompts below. Student A should ask the questions and Student B should answer them. Pay particular attention to the intonation.

1. pop music/classical music
2. adventure films/romantic films
3. Christmas/New Year
4. cars/motorbikes
5. studying/shopping

Listening

7a Listen to Peter and Maria talking about what entertainment they like and what they don't like. As you listen, complete the table below by putting a tick (✓) in the column for Peter or for Maria.

		Peter	Maria
1	watches TV a lot	☐	☐
2	prefers going out to staying in	☐	☐
3	loves live music	☐	☐
4	prefers classical music to pop music	☐	☐
5	goes to the cinema once or more a week	☐	☐
6	is fond of romantic films	☐	☐
7	hates romantic films	☐	☐
8	sometimes prefers to stay at home with a DVD	☐	☐

b Here are a number of expressions for saying how much you like or hate something. Put them in order from the most positive (1) to the most negative (6).

- A ☐ I can't stand…
- B ☐ I can't get enough of…
- C ☐ I really love…
- D ☐ I'm quite fond of…
- E ☐ …leaves me cold!
- F ☐ I don't mind…

c Now listen to Peter and Maria again. Tick (✓) the expressions in b) which they use.

d Work in pairs. Use the expressions from b) to talk about the types of entertainment that you like and don't like. Do you and your partner have similar tastes?

Entertainment & music

Reading

8a Work in pairs. Ask each other about what type of concert you most enjoy. Ask when your partner last went to a concert, and who was playing. Ask what your partner thought about the concert.

b Peter went to a concert recently and afterwards posted a short review of the concert on his blog. Read his review and find out what type of music was played.

c Now answer these questions.

1 Where was the concert?
2 What time did the concert start and finish?
3 Would Peter recommend the concert?

Writing

ISE → See ISE file on page 92

9a Now practise writing a review by answering the questions to complete the spaces below. You can make it as positive or as negative as you like!

b Read the text again and then, in your own words, write an email (100-130 words) to your English speaking friend:. You should:

- describe the Brighton singers' concert you went to
- explain which type of music you preferred.

From Bach to the Beatles

Last night the Brighton Festival Singers gave a concert at All Saints Church. The concert began at 8.00 p.m. and finished at 10.00, with a short interval. They were conducted by John Makepiece, who has conducted many major choirs in several European countries. The programme included works by Bach, Elvis Presley and the Beatles – as you can imagine there was something for everyone! The quality of the singing was very high and two pieces were accompanied beautifully by 18- year-old Jenny Wilkins on the piano. I really loved every minute! The choir was established in 1987 and consists of local singers who meet weekly to rehearse and prepare performances. Take the opportunity to go to their next performance!

Last night the group of the moment (What was the name of the group?) 1............................ performed at (Where was the concert?) 2........................ . The concert lasted for (How long did they play for?) 3........................ and they played all their hits, including (What is the name of one of their hits?) 4........................ . (Name of the group) 5........................ are from (Where are they from?) 6........................ . There are (How many people are there in the group?) 7........................ members in the group. The music they play is (What type of music do they play?) 8........................ . The atmosphere at the concert was (What was the atmosphere like?) 9........................ and the audience (What did the audience think of it?) 10........................ . The best part of last night's concert was (What was the best part of the concert?) 11........................, but the worst part was (What was the worst part?) 12........................ . Overall the concert (Was it a success?) 13........................ and I thought (What did you think about it?) 14........................ . In fact, (Would you recommend it?) 15........................ .

exam EXPERT

Topic phase
Responding to the examiner

The interview is divided into the following 4 parts:

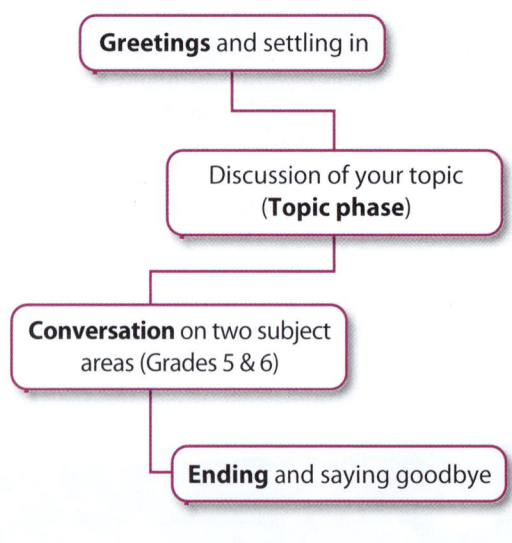

Before you start your topic the examiner will greet you, ask to see your photo identification and ask a few questions.

Asking the examiner questions

Be prepared to ask the examiner questions in the exam. At Grade 5 ask the examiner one question in the Topic phase and one question in the Conversation phase.
It is a good idea to prepare some possible questions to ask the examiner about your topic.

10a Match these questions and instructions (1-6) to the appropriate responses (A-F).

1. ☐ Please sit down.
2. ☐ What's your name?
3. ☐ How do you spell *Huang*?
4. ☐ How are you?
5. ☐ Can I have your Topic form, please?

A Lian Huang
B Fine thanks, and you?
C H-U-A-N-G
D Yes, of course. Here you are.
E Thank you.

b Now ask and answer the questions in a) with a partner.

11a Look at these example titles for a topic and think of two possible questions that you could ask the examiner for each one.

0 Football in Spain
   Is football popular in your country?
   Do you like watching football?

1 My home town
   ....
   ....

2 My trip to London
   ....
   ....

3 The Scouts
   ....
   ....

4 Canoeing
   ....
   ....

5 My hobby: karate
   ....
   ....

b Now write two questions that you could ask the examiner about your chosen topic.

30

exam EXPERT

Conversation
Exam practice

12a Match the questions (1-8) that an examiner might ask you about music and entertainment to suitable answers (A-I).

0 D Do you like listening to classical music?
1 ☐ What type of films do you enjoy watching?
2 ☐ How often do you go to the cinema?
3 ☐ Do you prefer watching films on TV or at the cinema?
4 ☐ Who is your favourite singer?
5 ☐ Have you seen any good films recently?
6 ☐ Which TV programme do you prefer watching?
7 ☐ How much TV do you watch every day?
8 ☐ Would you rather listen to pop music or reggae?

A I prefer watching films on the big screen.
B I love watching romantic films.
C I prefer Ed Sheeran because he's very talented.
D Yes, I love it because it's relaxing.
E At least once a month.
F I enjoy watching N.C.I.S.
G Not that much. About 2 hours a day.
H Yes, I've seen *Inception*. It's really good.
I I'd rather listen to reggae!

b With a partner, ask each other the questions above and give your own answers.

c Now think of a question that you could ask the examiner about music and entertainment.

Writing
ISE → See ISE file on pages 90 and 92

13 Choose one of these writing tasks.

An informal email
You have asked a friend to come with you to see your favourite band in concert. Write an email (100-130 words) to a friend. You should:
- explain why you prefer this band
- say why you think your friend will enjoy the concert.

A review
A new disco has recently opened in your area. Write a review (100-130 words) for an entertainment guide. You should:
- explain why you enjoyed your evening at the disco
- say how successful you think the disco will be.

Examiner: Can you play a musical instrument?
Candidate: No – but **I really love** listening to all types of music. How about you – are you a music lover, or **do you prefer** other forms of entertainment?

UNIT 4
Recent personal experiences

Vocabulary

1a Match the photos (A-H) with the activities (1-8) they show.

1. seeing friends
2. celebrating a special occasion
3. studying
4. playing video games
5. watching sport
6. going away for the weekend/on holiday
7. playing sport
8. going to a concert

b Tick (✓) three activities you like doing. Put a cross (✗) next to three you don't like doing. Compare your answers with a partner.

E.g. **A:** I really like going away for the weekend. What about you?

B: Yes, me too, especially in summer, to the beach. And I love going shopping! But I don't like watching sport. What about you?

A: Well, I don't like watching football, but I quite like watching tennis.

Recent personal experiences

■ **Past time expressions**

2a Read the posts from a social networking site about recent activities. Which activity from exercise 1a) does each person write about?

Alex writes:
I played in a match for the school team yesterday afternoon and we lost, 5-nil! We lost the weekend before last, too, by 6-nil! I think we need to train harder!

Ana writes:
I had such a great weekend! It was my mum's birthday last Saturday and we held a surprise party for her. It was so much fun! Check out the photos.

Jie writes:
They're over! I've finally finished. I did the last one yesterday. No more exams and no school for two months! All I've done for the past two weeks is revise! Now I can have some fun!

Shirin writes:
I want to live by the sea! We got back to town two hours ago, after a fantastic time at the beach. I miss it already!

Luca writes:
If you weren't there last night, you missed a fantastic experience. I think they played every song they've ever recorded. It was the best gig I've been to for ages.

b Underline the expressions relating to past time in the posts in exercise 2a).

c Complete the past time expressions in the table below using a word from the phrases you underlined in b).

d Jie uses the expression 'for two months' and Luca says 'for ages'. Does each person refer to the past, present or future? Can these expressions be used with other tenses?

3 Work with a partner. Ask and answer at least five questions about activities you've done recently. Use the expressions in the table below, where possible.

A: So, what did you do last night?
B: Nothing! I was so tired after last weekend, I went to bed at 9 o'clock!
A: Did you do anything last Saturday night?
B: Yes, actually, I went to a concert. It was great...

Remember!

I've finished my exams!
Use the Present Perfect to talk about events at an unspecified time in the past.

I *did* my French exam *yesterday*.
Use the Past Simple to talk about events that happened at a specified time in the past.

For more information on the use of the Present Perfect and Past Simple, see **Unit 1 page 10**.

1	night/week/weekend/month/year	
	Monday/Tuesday/Wednesday...	
the 2 ..../..............	two days/week/two weeks/two months/year	
the day/weekend/week/year	before 3	
4	morning/afternoon/evening	
two/three/four...	hours/days/weeks/months/years	5 ....

UNIT 4

Phonology

-ed past tense endings

4a Put the past tense forms in bold in these sentences from exercise 2a) into the correct column, according to the pronunciation of the -ed ending.

I **played** in a match for the school team yesterday afternoon and we lost, 5-nil!

They're over! I've finally **finished**.

I think they played every song they've ever **recorded**.

1	2	3
/t/	/d/	/ɪd/
	played	

b 🔊 Listen to check, then listen and repeat.

c 🔊 Now put these past tense forms into the correct columns. Listen to check, then listen and repeat.

> missed visited danced watched celebrated
> arrived decided wanted talked relaxed
> enjoyed loved worked waited

5a Work with a partner to invent a story.
- Use as many of the past verb forms from exercise 4c) as you can.
- Make notes, but don't write the story in full.
- Practise telling the story – remember the -ed endings!

b Change partners and tell your new partner your story.
- Count how many past verb forms from exercise 4c) your partner uses.
- Check your partner's pronunciation of the past tense verb forms.

Reading

6a Tick (✓) things (1-5) that you've bought and things (A-E) that you've done in the past six months. Then compare with a partner.

I've bought...
1. ☐ new clothes.
2. ☐ a computer.
3. ☐ an MP3 player.
4. ☐ a mobile phone.
5. ☐ a video game.

I've been...
A. ☐ on holiday.
B. ☐ to an adventure park.
C. ☐ for a meal at a restaurant.
D. ☐ to the cinema.
E. ☐ to visit a new place.

b What makes you feel happy? When you buy something, when you do something, or both? Compare your opinion with a partner.

Recent personal experiences

DOING OR BUYING?

A trip to an adventure park or a new MP3 player? A meal at a restaurant or a new pair of jeans? A smart new computer or a holiday? What would you choose?

Well, a study carried out in the USA by the University of Colorado has found that people are happier if they spend money on life experiences, rather than material possessions. Through a series of surveys and experiments over several years, researchers found that people from various social groups were happier when they spent money on doing things, rather than buying things.

One of the reasons suggested for this in the study is that experiences are more open to positive interpretations. For example, imagine you go on

a holiday and the weather or accommodation is not very good. Maybe you feel disappointed at the time, but later on, perhaps you'll change your view and start to think of the positive aspects of the experience – the new food you tried, or the new places that you saw. With material things, you can't reinterpret in this way because they are what they are – their qualities don't change.

Another possible reason why experiences bring more joy than material goods is that experiences also help us build up better social relationships. We tend to do things with other people, and we often share stories about the things we've done, so there is a social aspect to experiences that material possessions just don't have. And social success is closely associated with happiness.

7a Read the text above and answer these questions.

1 Is the text from
 A ☐ a science text book?
 B ☐ an article in newspaper or magazine?
 C ☐ an online advertisement?
2 What makes people the happiest, according to the article?
 A ☐ buying things
 B ☐ spending money
 C ☐ doing things

b Read the text again. Write T (true) or F (false) for each statement?

1 ☐ Research for the study took place in different countries.
2 ☐ The study lasted for a few months.
3 ☐ Lots of different kinds of people took part in the study.
4 ☐ According to the study, you can't change your opinion about experiences, but you can about material things.
5 ☐ According to the study, experiences help us develop socially, and this makes us happier.

8 Work with a partner. Tell her/him about:

1 a disappointing experience – how you felt at the time and how you felt later
2 something you've bought that made you feel really happy
3 something you've done with other people that's helped you socially.

UNIT 4

Grammar focus

Connecting clauses

We can connect clauses using words such as *because*, *but*, *so* and *also*. Look at these examples from the text and notice how the connecting words in bold are used.

A *Maybe you feel disappointed at the time,* **but** *later on, you may change your view...*
B *With material things, you can't reinterpret in this way* **because** *they are what they are...*
C *...experiences* **also** *help us build up better social relationships.*
D *...we often share stories about the things we've done,* **so** *there is a social aspect to experiences...*

9a Now match the sentences (A-D) to the explanations (1-4) about the use of the connecting word in each sentence.

1 ☐ to give reasons
2 ☐ to add a point
3 ☐ to make a contrasting point
4 ☐ to talk about results or consequences

b Match the beginnings (1-4) with the endings (A-D) to make sentences.

1 ☐ People like doing things with other people. They
2 ☐ Buying things can make people happy,
3 ☐ I'm not very happy with my new mobile phone
4 ☐ I spend all my time at work on a computer,

A because it's complicated to use.
B but doing things makes them happier.
C so I don't even want to check my email at weekends!
D also like talking about what they've done.

c Complete the sentences with a connecting word from the grammar focus.

1 I bought a new mobile phone .... my old one was broken.
2 We went to London last week and we .... went to Brighton.
3 My mum thinks this video game is too violent, ... she's taking it back to the shop.
4 Angela enjoyed the holiday, ... she didn't like the food very much.
5 I haven't got much money, ... I can't go on holiday this summer.

d Complete these sentences in your own words, then compare with a partner.

1 I like/don't like .... because ....
2 My favourite time of year is .... because ....
3 I really like/don't really like .... because ....
4 I'm happiest when I'm .... because ....

Writing

ISE ➔ See ISE file on page 89

10 Read the article on page 35 again, then, in your own words, write an article (100-130 words) to post on a blog about happiness. You should:

- explain what makes people happy
- give some examples of what makes you happy
- give reasons why these things make you happy.

exam EXPERT

Conversation
■ Showing understanding of the examiner

11a 🔊 Listen to the examiner and candidate talking in the Conversation phase. What subject area is the conversation about?

b 🔊 Listen again and tick (✓) the things that the examiner asks about.

0 ✓ activities/entertainment
1 ☐ location of the candidate's house
2 ☐ the candidate's family
3 ☐ transport
4 ☐ traffic problems
5 ☐ food and meals
6 ☐ details of the journey/s
7 ☐ the candidate's friends
8 ☐ the weather

c Match the examiner's questions to the topics discussed in b).

A ☐0☐ So, have you done anything special recently?
B ☐   Where is the house exactly?
C ☐   How did you get there?
D ☐   So, how long did the journey take?
E ☐   So was the weather good?
F ☐   Did you go to the beach?
G ☐   So, what do you prefer doing there?
H ☐   And did you do anything on the Saturday night?
I ☐   So, are you going to go there again next weekend?

d 🔊 Now match the candidate's answers to the questions in c). Then listen to the conversation again to check.

0 [C] By car – we usually prefer travelling in the family car, but this time it was terrible.
1 ☐ No, we probably won't go next weekend because the roads are so busy.
2 ☐ Oh, yes, I've been to our house at the seaside with my family. We went last weekend.
3 ☐ It's on the south-west coast, in a small village, about 200 km from here.
4 ☐ It took about seven hours!
5 ☐ Well, I like playing beach ball with my brother... and reading... but the thing I prefer doing is eating ice-cream!
6 ☐ Yeah, I went out for dinner with my family, then I met some friends...
7 ☐ Oh yes, it was beautiful – really hot and sunny all weekend.
8 ☐ Yes, we spent most of Saturday and Sunday on the beach. But I didn't swim very much because the sea was so cold.

e 🔊 The candidate asks the examiner a question. Listen to the end of the conversation again and complete the question.

And .... you – have you been .... for the .... recently?

f Use words and phrases from the box to make other questions that the candidate could ask the examiner. You can use some words and phrases more than once.

> Did you   anything special recently?
> travel here by plane?   D/do you   driving?
> like   What's   going to the beach?
> the weather   where you live?   Where
> live exactly?   the traffic   Have you
> done   lived in another country?

E.g.   Did you travel here by plane?

37

exam EXPERT

12a Read a candidate's answer to some questions about recent personal experience and guess what question the examiner asked the candidate. Then write some other questions.

1. I went away with my family.
   Have you been away anywhere recently? Who exactly ... ?
2. I went to India on holiday.
3. I went shopping.
4. I had exams at school.
5. I visited an old friend the day.
6. We celebrated my grandmother's birthday.

b Work with a partner. Have short conversations by asking each other your questions from exercise 12a) and inventing answers.

A: *Have you been away anywhere recently?*
B: *Yes, I have. I've been away with my family.*
A: *Really? When did you go?*
B: *We went last weekend.*
A: *And where did you go?*
B: *We went skiing in the mountains.*
A: *How nice!*

Conversation

■ **Exam practice**

13 Student A read the examiner rolecard and Student B read the candidate rolecard. Follow the instructions.

Student A: Examiner

Stage 1 Prepare questions to ask the candidate about a recent personal experience.

- Refer back to 11c) and 12a) for help with questions.

Stage 2 Have the conversation with Student B/the candidate.

Stage 3 Decide with Student B what went well in the conversation and what you could improve. Your teacher will also give you some ideas.

Stage 4 Now change roles and repeat stages 1-3.

Student B: Candidate

Stage 1 Think of something you've done recently and prepare to give details about it.

- Refer back to 11d) and 12a) for help.

Stage 2 Have the conversation with Student A/the examiner.

Stage 3 Decide with Student A what went well in the conversation and what you could improve. Your teacher will also give you some ideas.

Stage 4 Now change roles and repeat stages 1-3.

Writing

ISE ➡ *See ISE file on pages 87 and 90*

An informal email

You have just won a prize in a talent show for your singing. Write an email (100-130 words) to a friend. You should:

- explain what you had to do to win the prize
- say when you are planning to perform in the future.

A discursive essay

Write an essay (100-130 words) about social networking sites as a way of telling friends about your life and experiences. You should:

- say how you have used social networking sites
- explain how popular they will be in the future.

14 Choose one of these writing tasks to practise writing about recent personal experiences for the ISE I exam. Then follow stages A-H to do the task.

- **A** Refer to the Writing file for help with how to write the text type.
- **B** Refer to exercises in this unit for help with subject-area vocabulary and grammar.
- **C** Write a plan for your text.
- **D** Write a first draft.
- **E** Swap texts with a partner and suggest ways for your partner to improve her/his text.
- **F** Listen to what your partner says about how you can improve your text.
- **G** Write a second draft.
- **H** Give your text to your teacher.

Examiner: Have you done anything special recently?
Candidate: Yes, I have. I've celebrated my mother's birthday with my family. We went away for the weekend. We had a party outside because the weather was beautiful.

Review Units 1-4

1 The groups of letters below can be rearranged to make words we have used in the first two units. The first one has been done for you. Then, match the words to the definitions.

0	laminter	terminal
1	atunigorda	....
2	sontulieros	....
3	cyliceb	....
4	yawnur	....
5	yaBgniDox	....
6	derbi	....

A ☐ The ceremony that you attend when you have finished your studies at university.
B ☐ The word we use to describe a woman on her wedding day.
C ☐ The place where aircraft take off or land.
D ☒ The part of an airport where you find check-in desks, shops, restaurants etc.
E ☐ The promises that you make at the beginning of a New Year.
F ☐ The day after Christmas Day.
G ☐ Simple transport for one person with two wheels.

2 Here are a number of sentences. Some are right but some have a mistake in them. If you find a mistake, write the corrected sentence.

1 They are in Paris since last week.
2 I've been in this queue for hours!
3 I've seen him at the wedding last Saturday.
4 I play the guitar but I've never played it in public.
5 When I finished my studies I probably become a teacher.
6 The flight to Madrid will probably take two hours.

3 Use these words to make good sentences – you will need to add or change some words.

1 the Bull Run/Pamplona/happen/every year/1951
2 rocket/announce/bulls/leave
3 you/ever/eat/octopus?
4 often/travel/train?
5 she/just/finish/homework
6 I/probably/become/doctor/when/older
7 I/certain/they/arrive/here/an hour
8 I/go/Tokyo/1999/but/not be/there again

Review Units 1-4

4 Look again at the pictures of musical instruments on page 24. Now list the instruments in the table below next to the correct type of music. You can put some instruments in more than one row.

Jazz	
Pop	
Classical	
Folk	

5 Using some of the adjectives from the box on page 26, complete these sentences.

1 The film was really ....! In fact I thought it was never going to end!
2 It was the most .... film I've ever seen! I was sitting on the edge of my seat from the start to the finish!
3 She prefers .... films – you know, the type where a man falls in love with a woman and they are very happy!
4 I found the film really ....! I could guess exactly how it was going to end!

6 In the following sentences we have offered you two choices. Underline the correct word or phrase.

1 At last *I finished/I've finished* my exams. Now I'm free!
2 She prefers *swimming to skiing/to swim than to ski*.
3 I'd rather *to go/go* to the cinema.
4 She *visited/has visited* Turkey last year.
5 *Did you do/Have you done* anything special recently?

7 Read the information about the exam, and decide if they refer to the Topic phase (T), the Conversation phase (C), or both (TC).

1 ☐ It is the first part of the exam.
2 ☐ It lasts up to 5 minutes.
3 ☐ You must ask the examiner at least one question.
4 ☐ You mustn't memorise what you are going to say.
5 ☐ You must prepare a mind map with five discussion points on it.
6 ☐ It involves two subject areas.

Grade 5 Self-evaluation

Write Y (yes) or N (needs more practice) for each statement.

1 ☐ I can talk about festivals and celebrations.
2 ☐ I can talk about transport.
3 ☐ I can talk about films and entertainment.
4 ☐ I can talk about my preferences.
5 ☐ I can use the Present Perfect and Past Simple to talk about my experiences.
6 ☐ I can talk about the future using *will* for predicting and informing.
7 ☐ I can use words and phrases to connect clauses correctly.

UNIT 5
Fashion & money

GRADE 6

Vocabulary
■ **Fashion**

1a Label each picture with an expression from the box.

> high fashion   extreme fashion   street fashion
> unfashionable   old-fashioned

b With your partner ask and answer the following questions.

1 Which style do you think is the most attractive? Why?
2 Would you be happy to wear any of these clothes? Which ones?

c Now use these words to describe the people in the pictures.

> cool   sporty   scruffy   smart
> well-dressed   casual   fashionable

d Use the verbs below to complete the sentences.

> fit   match   suit   go with

1 That style really .... her, she always looks really good.
2 The jacket doesn't .... her, it's much too tight!
3 Those trousers he's wearing .... his jacket, in fact it's a suit.
4 Those brown shoes don't .... a T-shirt and shorts. Trainers are better.

Fashion & money

Listening

2a Imagine you have been invited to a friend's wedding. Talk to your partner about what you would wear.

1. Would you wear something fashionable / smart/unusual/casual/formal?
2. Would you wear a suit/a dress/a T-shirt and jeans?

b 🔊 Now listen to this conversation between Patricia and her boyfriend. Who knows most about what to wear – Patricia or Peter?

c 🔊 Listen again to the conversation. What does Patricia tell Peter to wear? Write Y (yes), N (no) and M (maybe) next to each photo.

d Look at the vocabulary in exercise 1c) again. Talk about these questions with a partner and try to use some of that vocabulary.

1. Ask your partner what plans she/he has for the weekend.
2. Ask him/her what he/she plans to wear.
3. Give your partner your opinions about their choice of clothes.

Phonology

Sentence stress to clarify meaning

3a 🔊 Listen to this sentence pronounced in two different ways. Which word, or words, is stressed in each sentence?

1. Would you like to try the jacket with a matching skirt, or a dress?

2. Would you like to try the jacket with a matching skirt or a dress?

🔊 Now listen to the two versions of the sentences again and repeat the stress patterns.

GRADE 6

UNIT 5

b 🔊 Now listen to these sentences and underline the stressed words. Tick the two options the shop assistant gives in each case.

1. Would you like to try the shirt with a tie, or a smart pullover?
   - A ☐ a shirt and a tie
   - B ☐ a pullover
   - C ☐ a shirt and a pullover
2. Would you like to try the long-sleeved shirt or T-shirt?
   - A ☐ a long-sleeved shirt
   - B ☐ a short-sleeved T-shirt
   - C ☐ a long-sleeved T-shirt

c 🔊 Now listen again and repeat.

Vocabulary

■ Money

4a Match the words (A-D) with their correct definitions (1-4).

- A ☐ a cheque
- B ☐ credit card
- C ☐ debit card
- D ☐ cash

1. you buy things with this small piece of plastic and pay for them the following month
2. your bank gives you these pieces of paper, which you can use to pay for things
3. real money – coins and notes
4. you get money from a machine and pay for things in shops with this small piece of plastic

b Work with a partner. Talk about these questions.

1. Which of these types of payment are common in your country?
2. Which one do you think is the most common?
3. Which type of payment do you usually use:
   - A ☐ in a shop?
   - B ☐ in a restaurant?
   - C ☐ on the Internet?
4. Are there any places where credit and debit cards are not accepted in your country?

5a How do you think European families spend their money in these five countries? In small groups, try to answer the questions below.

1. Where do you think people spend most on food?
2. Where do people spend least on education?
3. Which do you think are the top and bottom countries for spending on health?
4. Which country spends most on entertainment?

When you have guessed the right answers, go to page 95 and check if you were right.

Fashion & money

Grammar focus

Past Continuous

subject + *was/were* + verb + *-ing*
They **were talking** about the wedding.

We use the Past Continuous...

1 to describe past actions over a period of time.

*It was the day before the party. Francesca and Simon **were making** a cake and Isobel **was trying** to decide what to wear.*

*What **were** you **doing** last Friday?*

2 with the Past Simple to describe interrupted actions.

*He **was shopping** for a new suit when he **realised** that he didn't have his credit card.*

*She **was wearing** shorts and a T-shirt when it **started** raining.*

6a Complete these sentences using the Past Continuous form of a verb from the box.

> work eat run look stay talk

1 She .... to her friends about the party.
2 Steve .... his lunch when the phone rang.
3 .... (you) on the same project last year?
4 They .... in a cottage in France.
5 .... (Tom) when he fell over?
6 Daniel's family .... for a new house last year.

b Make sentences using the Past Continuous and Past Simple.

1 They/walk in park/dog escape
2 Megan/eat a sweet/tooth fall out
3 Mum/buy a new dress/see thief
4 Peter/phone ring/read newspaper
5 It/rain heavily/lights go out
6 We/shop online/steal credit card details

7 Now complete the gaps in this story with verbs in the Past Continuous or the Past Simple.

Last Saturday my friend Sarah and I **1**.................... shopping in the city centre. It was Juan's party that evening and we wanted to get something new to wear. We met at the bus stop at 10 o'clock but whilst we **2**.................... for the bus it **3**.................... raining and we didn't have an umbrella. We took the bus into the centre but we **4**.................... so much that we **5**.................... our stop and had to get off at the next one. We finally got to our favourite shop and Sarah **6**.................... the perfect dress for the party whilst I **7**.................... for a new jumper. She was so pleased... until she **8**.................... she didn't have her purse!

UNIT 5

Reading

8a Talk about these questions with another student.

1. What does *to tip* mean?
2. Have you ever worked in a place where you got tips? How did it make you feel?
3. Do you like giving tips? Are you generous or mean?

b Read the article below and find the words in the text that have these meanings:

1. impolite
2. the money you get paid each week for working
3. the piece of paper which tells you how much your meal has cost
4. well decorated and probably expensive

ADVICE ABOUT TIPPING IN ENGLAND

An American couple were eating dinner in a traditional pub restaurant during their trip to Britain last summer. As they were studying their bill at the end of the meal, they turned to a British man at the next table and asked him how much they should tip. He was confused and said, 'What tip?'. The American couple were looking at the man with surprise as they answered him, 'Well, some money for the waiter. Wouldn't it be rude not to leave a tip?'

Depending on where you are in the world, the unwritten 'rules' about tipping can be quite different. In America, for example, tips are considered to be compulsory, given that workers such as waiters, hairdressers and bar staff don't have very high wages. It is normal to add a 15% tip to the bill, or more if the service is particularly good.

In Britain tipping is more of a choice, depending on the kind of restaurant you are in and the quality of the service you receive. In an elegant restaurant a 10% tip is common, but if the service isn't good, then people generally won't leave a tip.

Fashion & money

c Look at the article carefully again and decide whether the following statements are true (T) or false (F).

1. ☐ Americans and British people feel the same way about tipping.
2. ☐ In Britain you must give tips in cheap cafès.
3. ☐ Some Americans might be too generous.
4. ☐ British people give tips even when the service is not good.

d Ask and answer the questions with a partner

1. In your country, who do you tip? e.g. hairdressers? waiters? taxi-drivers? ……
2. How much do you normally tip? e.g. 5%? 10%? it depends on…?
3. Are there people in your country that you don't tip – even though they get tips in other countries?

Writing

ISE → See ISE file on page 87

9 Read the article again and then, in your own words, write an essay (100-130 words) for your school magazine. You should:

- tell the reader about tipping in the US
- compare this with tipping in the UK
- say what you think about tipping.

exam EXPERT

Conversation

■ Preparing questions for the Conversation phase

Remember, in GESE and ISE examinations you have to talk **with** the examiner. This means that you have to answer the examiner's questions but you also have to **ask** some questions.

10 Complete the information about the Conversation phase using the words in the box.

examiner   one   all   question   two

In the Conversation phase of the Grade 6 exam you will have to speak about [1]………… of the subject areas from the syllabus. In the ISE I Conversation phase, you only have to speak about [2]………… of the subject areas. The [3]………… will choose which ones to talk about, so you need to be prepared to talk about [4]………… of them. You must ask the examiner at least one [5]………… about each subject area.

47

exam EXPERT

'Echo' questions
During natural conversations we often follow a pattern like this:

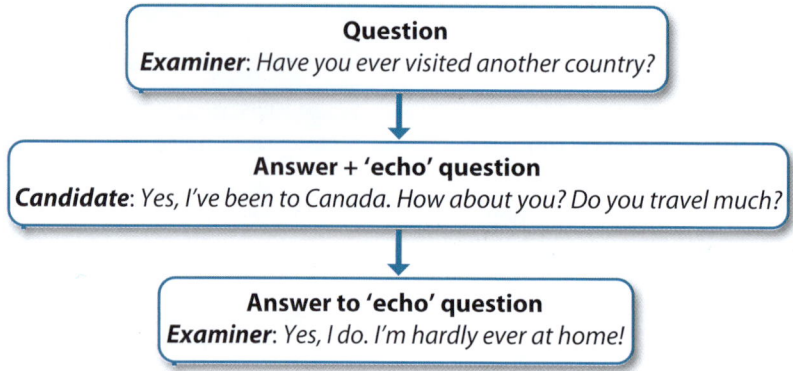

NB 'Echo' questions are about the same subject as the original question, but usually use different words.

11a Look at these other examples and complete the 'echo' question.

Conversation 1

Examiner: Are you interested in fashion?

Candidate: Well. not really, but my girlfriend loves fashionable clothes. How about you? ....?

Examiner: I'm more like you than like your girlfriend, I think!

Conversation 2

Examiner: Have you seen any good films lately?

Candidate: Yes. I've just seen *Harry Potter and the Deathly Hallows*. It was great! ....?

Examiner: Unfortunately, I just don't have enough time!

b Work with a partner. Take it in turns to be examiner and candidate and make short dialogues like these examples. Here are the questions for the 'examiners'.

1. Do you prefer travelling by train or plane?
2. When you travel do you like to use cash or a credit card?
3. Have you ever been to see an opera?
4. Have you been to a wedding or a birthday party recently?

exam EXPERT

Writing
ISE ➡ *See ISE file on pages 89 and 90*

12 Reorder the stages (A-H) for practising writing tasks for the ISE I exam.

- **A** ☐ Give your text to your teacher.
- **B** ☐ Write a first draft.
- **C** ☐ Write a plan for your text.
- **D** ☐ Write a second draft.
- **E** ☐ Refer to the Writing file for help with how to write the text type.
- **F** ☐ Listen to what your partner says about how you can improve your text.
- **G** ☐ Swap texts with a partner and suggest ways for your partner to improve her/his text.
- **H** ☐ Refer to exercises in this unit for help with subject area vocabulary and grammar.

13 Choose one of these writing tasks.

An informal mail
It is a friend's 18th birthday party soon. Another friend of yours has asked you about the party. Write an email (100-130 words) to answer your friend's questions about the party. You should:
- explain how your friend is celebrating the birthday
- say what you think you will wear to the party.

An article
Write an article (100-130 words) for a teenage magazine about young people's fashion. You should:
- give your opinion on the new styles
- say what clothes you think you might buy next.

Trinity TAKEAWAY

Examiner: If I go to a restaurant tonight, do I need to leave a tip? How much?
Candidate: It really depends on the service you get. If it's good, you need to give about 10% of the bill. Do you normally give tips in England?

UNIT 6
Travel

Vocabulary

1a Match the names (1-7) with the continents (A-G) on the map.

1. ☐ Africa
2. ☐ Antarctica
3. ☐ Asia
4. ☐ Australia
5. ☐ Europe
6. ☐ North America
7. ☐ South America

b 🔊 Listen to the names of the continents from a) and mark the stress.

E.g. Africa

c 🔊 Listen again and repeat.

2 Work with a partner. Look at the photos and say where you think the places are.

E.g. I think Picture 1 is in Asia. What do you think?

Focus	
To express an opinion, say:	
I think	it/Picture 1/he etc. **'s/is**...
	they/the pictures etc. **'re/are**...
To request an opinion, say:	
What do you think?	

Travel

3a Match the words (A-D) with their definitions (1-4).

A travel (verb)   C trip (noun)
B journey (noun)   D travelling (noun)

1 ☐ the action of going from one place to another
2 ☐ the activity of visiting different places
3 ☐ when you go from one place to another
4 ☐ when you go to a place, usually for a short time, and come back again

b Complete these sentences with travel words from a).

1 .... is a good way to meet new people.
2 I .... a lot for my job, so I prefer to stay at home in my free time.
3 I want to go .... around the world after I finish university.
4 My .... to school is very quick – I can walk there in five minutes.
5 Our .... to New York was great. We only had three days there, but we saw so much.
6 The .... from London to Paris by train takes less than two and a half hours.

b Now look back at the photos on page 50 and, using words and phrases from a), say:

- what type of holiday is shown.
- what people do on this type of holiday.
- what type of accommodation people stay in.
- how people travel in this type of place.
- why people go to the type of place in the photos (see **Focus** box).

Focus
To express purpose, say: *I'm **going to** the beach **to relax**.* *He **went** shopping **to buy** a new pair of shoes.* *People **go to** Paris **to see** the famous sights.*

4a Work with a partner. Write the words and phrases from the box in the correct column.

> the mountains   a lake   backpacking
> camping   a cruise   by plane   by boat/ferry
> self-catering (apartment, villa)   a tent
> the countryside   sunbathing   going sightseeing
> walking   bed and breakfast (B&B)
> a package holiday   relaxing   by train
> a city   a beach holiday   a hotel   doing sport
> the seaside   an activity holiday   by car
> a youth hostel   the desert

holiday types	places	accommodation	activities	transport
a cruise	the mountains	a hotel	going sightseeing	by train

GRADE 6

51

exam EXPERT

Conversation
■ Examiner and candidate roleplay

5a Student A read the examiner role card and Student B read the candidate role card. Follow the instructions.

Student A: Examiner

Stage 1 Prepare questions to ask the candidate (Student B) about holidays:

- find out your partner's opinions on different types of holiday.
- try and make some questions using the present perfect (G5); *prefer* (G5); *why* (G5); *must, might, need to, have to* (G6); zero and first conditionals (G6).
- use the categories in exercise 4a) when planning your questions.

Stage 2 Have the conversation with Student B.

Stage 3 Decide with Student B what went well in the conversation and what you could improve. Your teacher will also give you some ideas.

Student B: Candidate

Stage 1 The examiner (Student A) is going to ask you some questions about holidays. To prepare:

- think about the type of holidays you like and don't like and why.
- be prepared for some questions using the present perfect (G5); *prefer* (G5); *why* (G5) *must, might, need to, have to* (G6); zero and first conditionals (G6).
- use the vocabulary in exercises 1, 2, 3 and 4 when planning your answers.

Stage 2 Have the conversation with Student A.

Stage 3 Decide with Student A what went well in the conversation and what you could improve. Your teacher will also give you some ideas.

'Holidays' isn't a subject area in the Conversation phase but this is useful practice for talking about travel and money, which are subject areas for Grade 6

b Now change roles and repeat stages 1-3.

6a Read the blog posts (1-4) about holiday plans. What type of holiday does each person write about?

b Work with a partner. Tell each other which of the four trips you'd prefer to take and why.

c Underline phrases with the Present Continuous for future use and expressions relating to future time in the blog posts.

1 Louise, London, UK
At the end of July, I'm going on holiday for two weeks with some friends, to Spain. We're staying in an apartment at the seaside, on the Costa Brava, north of Barcelona. I can't wait!

2 Pierre, Bordeaux, France
I'm not really having a holiday this summer. I'm spending all of August studying English, in Brighton, on the south coast of England. I'm leaving on 31st July and coming back to France on 1st September. ☹

3 Jim, Seattle, USA
I'm going on a really cool trip in June. I'm going with my parents and my brother on a trip to Tanzania, in Africa, on a safari! It's going to be amazing!

4 Marina, Madrid, Spain
Well, I'm not really going on holiday this summer, but I am going away. I'm leaving at the beginning of August and coming back in a year's time! I'm going with a friend, and we're travelling around North and South America for a year, by train.

Travel

Grammar focus

Present Continuous for future use

To talk about fixed future plans, use:
am/are/is (not) + **verb** + *-ing* (Present Continuous) + **future time expression**.

At the end of July, I**'m going** on holiday for two weeks with some friends, to Spain.
I**'m not** really **having** a holiday **this summer**.
I**'m leaving at the beginning of August** and **coming back in a year's time**!
Are you **working the day after tomorrow**?

- When speaking, and in informal writing, we use the contractions *'m/'re/'s* instead of *am/are/is*.
- The future time expression can go at the beginning or end of the sentence.
- Sometimes the Present Continuous is used to talk about fixed future plans without the future time expression. This is because the time reference is implicit and/or has probably been mentioned already.
  E.g. *We're staying* in an apartment at the seaside…
  I'm going with a friend…

7a Complete the sentences using information from the blog posts in exercise 6a).

1. Louise .... on holiday for two weeks at .... She .... in an apartment on the Costa Brava.
2. Pierre .... a real holiday this .... He .... all of .... studying English. He .... France on 31st July.
3. Jim .... on a trip to Africa with his parents, in ....
4. Marina .... at the .... August. She .... with a friend around North and South America for a year.

b Work with a partner. Ask and answer questions about future plans.

Questions	
Are you doing anything	next weekend?
What are you doing	next summer?
	on Saturday evening?
	the day after tomorrow?
	in a year's time?
	at Christmas? etc.

Answers
I'm playing in a basketball match next weekend.
No, I'm not doing anything. I haven't got any plans.

Follow-up questions
What about you?
And you? Are you doing anything on/at/in/for…?

c Now change partners. Tell your new partner about three of your previous partner's future plans.

UNIT 6

Reading

8a Work with a partner. Look at the photos and answer the questions.

1. What type of holiday do the photos show?
2. Would you like to go on a holiday like this? Why/Why not?

b With your partner, make a list of ways in which tourists on this type of holiday can save money on eating, travel and sightseeing.

E.g. **0** *Buy a young person's travelcard.*

9a Read the advice from an article about how young travellers can save money. Match the paragraphs (1-6) to the categories (A-C).

A eating ..4.. ....
B travel ....
C sightseeing ......

b Now complete the article with the verbs from the box.

> buy   check (x2)   drink   eat (x2)   keep
>   take (x2)   walk   waste

c Work with a partner. Read the article again and answer the questions.

1. Are any of the points in the article the same as the ones on your list in exercise 8b?
2. Do you agree with all the advice for travellers in the article? Why/Why not?

TRAVEL ON THE CHEAP

1. ¹............ with the local tourist office if there are any special visitors' cards that will save you entrance fees at museums and attractions. Also, ask when or if museums and galleries have free openings.

2. ²............ whenever possible instead of paying for buses or the underground, and ³............ the cost of public transport if choosing a hostel or B&B out of town.

3. ⁴............ a Travelcard for the buses/trams/underground if staying long enough to make it worthwhile (bring passport photos from home).

4. If you are staying in accommodation where breakfast is included, ⁵............ enough to keep you going for the day. This way, you can save money on lunch bills.

5. If you do get hungry during the middle of the day, set menus at lunchtime are far better value than dinner, so ⁶............ your main meal as a late lunch. And in Mediterranean countries, do as the locals do and ⁷............ your coffee at the bar – it costs a lot more to sit down.

6. If you are travelling by train or coach, ⁸............ a picnic with you. Don't ⁹............ valuable cash on expensive, poor quality railway or motorway service station food. ¹⁰............ a plastic water bottle and ¹¹............ re-filling it when you can.

exam EXPERT

Writing

ISE ➡ *See ISE file on pages 88 to 90*

10 Choose one of these writing tasks to practise writing about travel for the ISE I exam. Then follow stages A-H to do the task.

An email or letter
A friend is coming to visit your country. Write an email or letter (100-130 words) to your friend. You should:
- explain how your friend will be able save money on travel in your country
- say how you think you friend can save money on food.

An article
Write an article (100-130 words) for a travel magazine with the title 'The importance of foreign travel'. You should:
- explain why it is important to visit foreign countries
- describe what you have learnt from your own experience of travel.

A descriptive essay
Write an essay for a website about the worst journey you have ever had. You should:
- say where you were travelling to
- explain why the journey was so bad.

A Refer to the ISE file on pages 87-92 for help with how to write the text type.
B Refer to exercises in this unit for help with subject-area vocabulary and grammar.
C Write a plan for your text.
D Write a first draft.
E Swap texts with a partner and suggest ways for your partner to improve her/his text.
F Listen to what your partner says about how you can improve your text.
G Write a second draft.
H Give your text to your teacher.

exam EXPERT

Topic phase

11a 🔊 Listen to Beatriz, a candidate from Spain, talking about her topic with the examiner. Number the points on her Topic form below in the order she mentions them.

b 🔊 Listen again and tick (✓) the extra questions that the examiner asks.

1. ☐ And who do you go with?
2. ☐ Have you got any friends there?
3. ☐ How long have your grandparents lived there?
4. ☐ So, when are you next going there?
5. ☐ What's it called again?
6. ☐ What's your favourite place in the village?

c 🔊 Listen again and underline the correct word or phrase.

0. Beatriz's favourite place is in the <u>mountains</u>/city.
1. The examiner has a problem understanding the name/location of Beatriz's favourite place.
2. Beatriz goes to the village to ski/enjoy the scenery.
3. Beatriz's grandparents have lived there for a short/long time.
4. Beatriz has been to her favourite place a lot/only a few times this year.
5. Beatriz prefers travelling to the village by car/by bus.
6. If Beatriz has a holiday from university, she goes to another country/the village.
7. If you go to the ski station, you must/don't need to be able to ski.
8. Beatriz will/might live in the village in the future.

d 🔊 Listen to the first part of the recording again and complete the questions that Beatriz asks the examiner.

And …………… …………… you? …………… …………… favourite place?

☐ How often I go there

0 Location

☐ Plans for the future

My favourite place

☐ Why I go there

☐ How I prefer to travel

☐ What people must see there

exam EXPERT

12 Complete the exam advice with the words *Do* or *Don't*.

Topic – Dos and Don'ts

1 <u>Don't</u> choose a topic that you're not interested in or don't know much about.
2 .... prepare a monologue for the topic. The examiner doesn't want you to just repeat a speech you've learnt.
3 .... expect to be asked about your topic in the order of the points on the Topic form.
4 .... complete the correct number of points on your Topic form – 6 for Grade 6 and ISE I.
5 .... prepare enough material to talk for up to five minutes.
6 .... ask the examiner at least one question on the subject of your topic.
7 .... bring pictures, photos, diagrams, models, maps, or other suitable objects to the exam, if you think they will help the discussion.
8 .... bring anything that's alive to the exam, e.g. insects or animals!

13a Student A read the examiner role card and Student B read the candidate role card. Follow the instructions.

Student A: Examiner

Stage 1 Prepare questions to ask the candidate (Student B) about a favourite place:
- Use the points for discussion from Beatriz's Topic form to help you think of things to ask.
- Try and use some language of the grade.
- When Student B is ready, take her/his Topic form.

Stage 2 Ask Student B questions about the topic. Answer the question that she/he asks you.

Stage 3 Decide with Student B what went well in the presentation and what you could improve. Your teacher will also give you some ideas.

Student B: Candidate

Stage 1 Prepare a topic presentation about your favourite place.
- Use the discussion points from Beatriz's Topic form to help you think of what to say.
- Try and use some language of the grade.
- Prepare your own topic form with points suitable for your topic.
- Give your Topic form to Student A.

Stage 2 Talk about your topic with Student A. Remember to ask the examiner a question.

Stage 3 Decide with Student A what went well in the presentation and what you could improve. Your teacher will also give you some ideas.

b Now change roles and repeat stages 1-3.

Trinity TAKE AWAY

Examiner: What types of holidays do you like best?
Candidate: I enjoy lots of different types of holiday, but I prefer going on beach holidays. The type of holiday I can't stand is camping.

UNIT 7
Learning a language; Rules & regulations

GRADE 6

 A
 B
 C
 D
 E
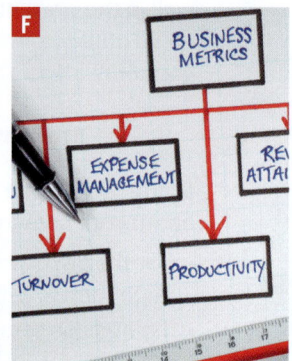 F
 G
 H

Vocabulary

■ Learning a language

1a Match the photos (A-H) showing different ways of learning a foreign language with the phrases (1-8).

1. ☐ reading books, newspapers and magazines
2. ☐ listening to/watching things on the Internet
3. ☐ going to classes
4. ☐ having private lessons
5. ☐ studying with friends outside of class
6. ☐ living and working in a country where the language is spoken
7. ☐ learning lots of grammar and vocabulary
8. ☐ studying at school in the foreign language

b Work with a partner. Ask and answer the questions.

1. Which do you think are the three best ways in exercise 1a) to learn a language? Give reasons.
2. Which of these ways of learning a language have you tried? Which do you want to try in the future?

E.g. I think having private lessons is a good way to learn a language, because the teacher can give you lots of attention.

I want to live in Australia when I'm older, to learn English there.

Learning a language; Rules & regulations

Reading

2a Read the tips from an article about language learning and match the headings (A-D) with the paragraphs (1-4).

- A Errors
- B Listening
- C Reading
- D Understanding

b Work with a partner. Ask and answer these questions.

1 Which do you think is the most useful tip? Give reasons.
2 Which do you think is the most difficult tip to follow? Give reasons.

E.g. *I think the tip about errors is really useful. I worry too much about making mistakes!*

3 Match the phrases in bold (1-9) in the text in exercise 2a) with their function (A-D).

A It's necessary to do ....
B It's not necessary to do ....
C It's necessary **not** to do ....
D It's possible, but not certain ...2.... ....

Learning a Language

Are you studying hard, but not making much progress? Are you thinking: ¹ *What do I have to do to really learn a language?* Follow these tips to find out.

1 ☐ You won't understand everything – in fact, at the beginning of the learning process, ² **you might not understand much at all**. But ³ **you need to accept** that ⁴ **you don't have to understand everything** to be able to communicate.

2 ☐ To learn a language, you have to practise it. This means ⁵ **you have to speak** – and sometimes to write. And when you're speaking and writing you will make mistakes, but ⁶ **you mustn't get demotivated** by this. Instead, learn from the mistake you make – how can I say that correctly? – and ⁷ **next time, you might get it right!**

3 ☐ This is an essential aspect of learning a language – ⁸ **you need to hear other people speaking it to be able to speak it yourself**. You can get lots of material from the Internet – videos, podcasts, news broadcasts. Put it on your MP3 player and practise this skill wherever you go.

4 ☐ This really helps with learning a foreign language, but ⁹ **you must choose things that you're interested in**. So, if you love photography, get a magazine about photography, or print out an article about it from the Internet in the language you're trying to learn.

UNIT 7

Grammar focus

Expressing obligation, necessity and uncertainty

1 To express obligation and necessity, use *must*, *have to* and *need to* + infinitive.
...you **need to hear** other people speaking.
...you **have to speak**.
...you **must choose** things that you're interested in.

2 To express lack of obligation, use *don't (do not)/doesn't (does not) have to* + infinitive.
...you **don't have to understand** everything to be able to communicate.

3 To express negative obligation, use *musn't (must not)* + infinitive.
...you **mustn't get** demotivated by this.

4 To express uncertainty, use: *might/might not* + infinitive.
...you **might not understand** much at all.

5 To ask questions about obligation or rules, use *do/does* + subject + *have to* + infinitive.
What **do I have to do to** really learn a language?

4a Complete the sentences with language to express obligation, necessity and uncertainty from the box.

1. I .... do two hours' homework every afternoon – it's too much!
2. You .... revise for your English exam – you failed your last one!
3. We .... go to London for New Year, but we're not sure – my Mum doesn't know if she .... work or not.
4. You .... play music after 11p.m., because I can't sleep if there's noise.
5. He .... study very hard, he passes his exams easily without studying!
6. What time .... start school in the morning?
7. I speak some Spanish, but I'm worried that I .... understand anything when I go to Peru on holiday.
8. .... study a lot to learn Chinese?

b Work with a partner to answer these questions about your native language/s.

1. Do many people from other countries speak your language? Do some nationalities tend to speak your language better than others? Why do you think this is?
2. What aspects of your language are easy to learn?
3. What aspects of your language are difficult to learn?
4. Make a list of what someone has to do to really learn your language well.

E.g.

Valeria, Italy
'It's easy to learn to read Italian, because there are clear rules for how to pronounce the letters. Not like in English!'

Anthi, Greece
'Having to learn a different alphabet can make Greek difficult for people to learn.'

c Change partners and compare your lists from exercise 4b) question 4.

Learning a language; Rules & regulations

Phonology

■ **Connected speech at sentence level: stress and weak forms**

5a 🔊 Listen to these sentences from the article on page 59 and mark the stress in each one.

0   You might not understand much at all.
1   You don't have to understand everything.
2   You mustn't get demotivated.
3   You need to hear other people speaking.
4   You must choose things that you're interested in.
5   What do I have to do to really learn a language?

b 🔊 Listen and repeat the sentences from a).

c 🔊 Listen to some more sentences and write in the box the number of words that you hear. Contractions count as two words.

1   ☐   ....
2   ☐   ....
3   ☐   ....
4   ☐   ....
5   ☐   ....

d 🔊 Listen again and write the sentences you hear.

e 🔊 Listen and repeat the sentences from d).

Vocabulary

■ **Rules and regulations**

6a Work with a partner and answer these questions.

1   What do the signs (1-14) below show that you mustn't do?
2   Where would you see these signs?
3   Do you agree that it's a good idea to stop people doing these things? Give reasons.

E.g. Number 1 shows that you mustn't take photos. You might see this in an art gallery.
Yes, I think it's a good idea to stop people doing this, because the camera flash can damage the paintings.

b Make a list in the table of the rules and regulations in your life.

at home:
I have to make my bed in the mornings.

at school/work:
I have to wear a uniform to school.

in the public places I go to:
I have to wear a hat in the swimming pool.

UNIT 7

c Work with a partner. Using your list from b), to ask and answer questions about the rules and regulations in your life, at home, at school/work and in public places. Say how you feel about each one.

E.g. **A:** Do you have to make your own bed?
B: No, my Dad does it for me! I'm lucky.
A: Do you have to wear a school uniform?
B: Yes, and I hate it!

7 Work in groups of three or four and follow these instructions.

1. Talk about the schools you go to, or went to in the past, the rules and regulations that they have/had and how you would like to change them.
2. Write a list of rules for a perfect school.
3. Present your rules to the class.
4. Vote to decide which group has the most perfect school.

8a Complete the text about strange laws around the world with the countries in the box.

*Arkansas, USA   Athens, Greece   Britain (x4)
Florida, USA   France   Miami, USA
Singapore   Vermont, USA*

b Now, go to page 95 and check your answers.

c Work with a partner. Ask and answer these questions.

1. Which do you think is the strangest law above?
2. Which is the least strange law?
3. What reasons could there be behind each law?

E.g. I think they're all very stange, but, for me, the one about the whale is the strangest!

Does it feel like your life is full of rules? That people are telling you what to do at home, at school, in the street – wherever you go? Well, if you think that there are too many rules where you live, check out these weird and wonderful laws from around the world.

1. In ...., it's illegal to skateboard in a police station.
2. In ...., it's illegal to chew chewing gum.
3. It's illegal to die in the Houses of Parliament in ....
4. In ...., it's illegal to put a stamp with the head of the British queen upside down on a letter.
5. In ...., you can't call a pig Napoleon.
6. In ...., unmarried women who parachute on Sundays can be put in prison.
7. In ...., women must get written permission from their husbands to wear false teeth.
8. In .... if a dead whale is found on the coast, the head is legally the property of the king and the tail of the queen.
9. In ...., the police can take your driving licence away if they think your are badly dressed or aren't clean.
10. In ...., it's illegal for a woman getting married for the second time to wear a white wedding dress.
11. In ...., all swans are owned by the queen and it's illegal to hunt them.

Learning a language; Rules & regulations

Writing

ISE → See ISE file on page 89

9 Using ideas from the text on page 62, in your own words, write an article (approximately 100-130 words) for your school online magazine. You should:

- give examples of the strange laws in different countries, including examples from your own country if you know any
- say what you think are the reasons behind the laws
- describe a law in your country that you think needs to change.

exam EXPERT

10a Work with a partner. Match the punishments (1-6) with their definitions (a-f).

1. ☐ get detention
2. ☐ get lines
3. ☐ be suspended
4. ☐ be expelled

A when you have to leave your school

B when you have to stay in the classroom at break time or after school and possibly do extra work

C when you have to write a sentence repeatedly

D when you're not allowed to go to school for a period of time

b With your partner, discuss what punishments you would get in a school in your country for:

- talking in class
- fighting
- not doing your homework
- being rude to a teacher
- not wearing the correct school uniform
- wearing too much make-up or jewellery
- smoking

11a 🔊 Listen to Richard talking about punishments in schools in the UK. As you listen, make notes about at least six things that he mentions.

b Listen to the talk again. As you listen, check your notes and add to them as necessary.

c Work with a partner. Compare your information from stages a and b. Work together to try and remember what Richard said.

12 Work with a partner and answer the questions.

1. Do you think that corporal punishment is a good way of dealing with seriously bad behaviour in schools? Why / Why not?
2. What do you think is the most effective way of punishing a child for something they do wrong, at school or at home?

exam EXPERT

Conversation phase

13a Work with a partner and follow these instructions.

1. Make a list of the different aspects of the subject of 'rules and regulations' the examiner could ask you about in the Conversation phase. Refer to exercises 6, 7, 8 and 10 for help.

   e.g. rules about school

2. Now prepare some questions – at least five – to ask about each of the aspects on your list and think about how the candidate could answer the questions.

   e.g. Do you have to wear school uniform?

3. Prepare two questions that the candidate could ask the examiner about rules and regulations.

   e.g. Did you have to wear school uniform when you were at school?

b One of you is Student A, the other Student B. Student A read the examiner rolecard and Student B read the candidate rolecard. Follow the instructions.

Student A: Examiner

Stage 1 Have a conversation with the candidate (Student B) about rules and regulations. Use the questions you prepared above. Answer the questions that the candidate asks you.

Stage 2 Decide with Student B what went well in the conversation and what you could improve. Your teacher will also give you some ideas.

Student B: Candidate

Stage 1 Have a conversation with the examiner (Student A) about rules and regulations. Remember to ask the examiner at least two questions.

Stage 2 Decide with Student A what went well in the conversation and what you could improve. Your teacher will also give you some ideas.

c Now change roles and repeat Stages 1-2.

14 Repeat exercise 13a-c, this time to practise talking about the subject of 'learning a language' in the Conversation phase.

exam EXPERT

Writing

ISE → See ISE file on pages 88 and 90

15 Choose one, or more, of these writing tasks. Follow the stages (A-H) to help you.

A descriptive essay

Write an essay (100-130 words) for your school magazine about rules teenagers have to follow in your country. You should:
- give your opinion of some of these rules
- explain what happens if someone breaks these rules.

An informal email

A friend from another country is planning to hire a car while on holiday in your country. Write an email (100-130 words) to your friend. You should:
- say what the most important driving rules are
- explain what will happen if your friend does not follow the rules..

A Refer to the ISE file for help with how to write the text type.
B Refer to exercises in this unit for help with subject area vocabulary and grammar.
C Write a plan for your text.
D Write a first draft.
E Swap texts with a partner and suggest ways for your partner to improve her/his text.
F Listen to what your partner says about how you can improve your text.
G Write a second draft.
H Give your text to your teacher.

Examiner: What do you **have to do** to learn a foreign language well?
Candidate: I think you **have to** listen a lot, and practise speaking as much as you can. You **mustn't** get demotivated when you make mistakes – they **might** help you to get it right next time!

UNIT 8
Health & fitness

How much do you know about health and fitness? Do this quiz to find out.

1 How many litres of water do you need to drink every day to keep healthy?
 A a litre
 B two litres
 C half a litre

2 To stay fit, you need to exercise for at least
 A 20 minutes two or three times a week.
 B an hour two or three times a week.   C 10 minutes two or three times a week.

3 For a healthy diet, you need to eat fruit and/or vegetables at least
 A twice a week.
 B five times a day.
 C once a day.

4 If you want to sleep well, don't drink coffee   A after 8 p.m.   B after 3 p.m.   C after midday.

5 You need to eat fish
 A two or three times a month.
 B five times a day.
 C two or three times a week.

6 Which food has fat that is good for you?
 A margarine
 B extra virgin olive oil
 C chips

7 To help solve a problem that's causing you stress,
 A try to forget about it.   B take medicine for it.
 C talk about it with people.

8 The biggest preventable cause of death and disease in the world is
 A smoking.   B AIDS.   C stress.

Health & fitness

Vocabulary
■ Health and fitness 1

1a Circle the answers (A-C) you think are correct in the quiz, then compare with a partner.

b 🔊 Listen to a radio presenter giving the answers to the quiz questions and tick (✓) the correct answers.

c 🔊 Listen again and match the phrase/s (A-H) with the quiz questions on page 66. Some phrases relate to more than one question.

A	☐	10 million deaths
B	☐	wait for 24 hours
C	☐	having more energy
D	☐	stopping depression
E	1	keeping your heart healthy
F	☐	preventing some cancers
G	☐	something not to do after lunch
H	☐	vitamins and minerals your body needs

d Now tell a partner:
- how many of your answers from a) are correct.
- if there are any facts or statistics in the quiz that surprised you.
- which of the things in the quiz you do to keep healthy – or don't do!

Focus	
To express surprise, you can say:	
That	
It	*was a surprise* to me.
etc.	
I *was surprised* about	this.
	that.
	etc.

E.g. I was surprised about the answer to question 1 – I never drink that much water in a day.

The answer to question 4 was a surprise to me – I always have a coffee before I go to bed.

e 🔊 Complete the sentences from the recording in exercise 1, then listen again to check. Compare your answers with a partner.

1. If you .... to be healthy, you .... to drink at least two litres of water per day...
2. If you .... more water, you .... less chance of getting heart disease...
3. ...if you .... caffeine in the afternoon, it .... stop you sleeping at night.
4. ...when you .... about the problem to someone, you .... better...

UNIT 8

Grammar focus

Zero conditional

To express certainty about the consequences of a situation; to talk about a fact – something that is always true, use:

if/when + present verb form   present verb form
If you **want** to be healthy, you **need** to drink at least two litres of water per day.

First conditional

To express certainty and possibility about the consequences of a present or future situation, use:

if/when + present verb form   *will/will not* (or *may/may not*) + infinitive
If you **drink** more water, you'**ll have** less chance of getting heart disease.
If you **drink** caffeine in the afternoon, it **may stop** you sleeping at night.

If you're sure about the consequence, use **will/won't**.
If you're not so sure, use **may/may not**.

When speaking, and in informal writing, we use these contractions:
- *'ll = will*
- *won't = will not*

The clause with **'ll/won't** (or **may**) + infinitive can also go first, with *if* + present verb form as the second clause.

2a Complete the conditional sentences using the words in brackets.

0   If people ..*eat*.. (*eat*) lots of fast food, it ..*'s*.. (*be*) bad for their health.

1   If she .... (*talk*) to someone about her problems, I'm sure she .... (*feel*) better.

2   You .... (*not sleep*) very well tonight if you .... (*have*) a cup of coffee now. It's 9 p.m.

3   If you .... (*drink*) lots of water, you .... (*have*) less chance of getting some cancers.

4   If he .... (*eat*) chips every day, he .... (*put on*) weight. It's very simple!

5   When people .... (*eat*) less and .... (*do*) exercise, they .... (*lose*) weight.

6   They eat a lot of butter. If they .... (*use*) extra virgin olive oil instead, they .... (*be*) healthier.

7   We .... (*not go*) to the party if we .... (*not find*) a babysitter.

8   When she .... (*come*) back from her holiday, she .... (*phone*) me, I'm sure.

b Work in pairs. Write a list of ten points on how people can be healthier and fitter. Use information from the previous two pages and ideas of your own.

E.g.   If you exercise twice a week, for at least twenty minutes, you'll be fitter.

c Compare your list with another pair's. Are any of your points the same?

Health & fitness

Phonology
Intonation at sentence level

3a 🔊 Listen to a fitness instructor giving advice about keeping fit. As you listen to the advice, complete the information below.

1. It helps if ....
2. If you don't have a good diet, ...
3. If you do some exercise, ...
4. When you exercise, ...
5. You'll have less chance of getting heart disease if ....
6. If you exercise twice a week, ...
7. It'll be more fun ....
8. If you want to stay healthy, ...

b What do you notice about the instructor's voice at the end of each sentence?

c 🔊 Now listen again and repeat the sentences.

b 🔊 Listen and repeat the words from a).

c Now use the words to complete the sentences.

1. I think I need stronger glasses. I'll make an appointment with the .... for an eye test next week.
2. My tooth hurts. I need to see a ....
3. The person that a doctor treats is called a ....
4. I've hurt my back – I think I need some sessions with a .... to make it better.
5. The .... is closed at weekends – if you need to see a doctor then, you have to go to the hospital.
6. My stay in hospital wasn't too bad – one very kind .... even brought me a cup of tea in the middle of the night!
7. When you go to the ...., can you buy me some aspirin?
8. I don't think you need to see a doctor – you can ask the .... to suggest some medicine to buy.

Vocabulary
Health and fitness 2

4a Match the healthcare words in the box with the people and places in the photos (A-F).

1. chemist's/pharmacy
2. dentist
3. nurse
4. optician
5. physiotherapist
6. surgery

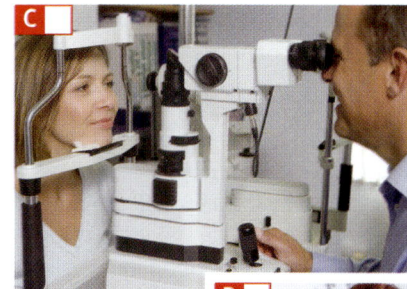
C

A

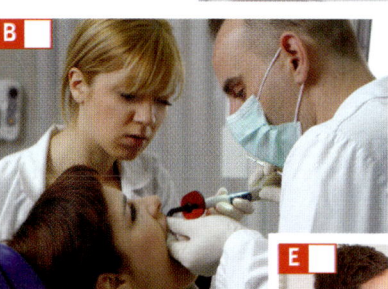
B

D

E

F

UNIT 8

Reading

5a Which healthcare services are free in your country? Which do you pay for? With a partner, make a list:

b Read the information about some of the healthcare services that are available free in Britain with the National Health Service (NHS). Are they the same as your list of free services in a)?

c Read the information again and match the headings (A-D) to the paragraphs (1-4).

- A NHS Direct online
- B NHS walk-in centres
- C Dental access centres
- D GP surgeries

ACCESSIBLE HEALTHCARE

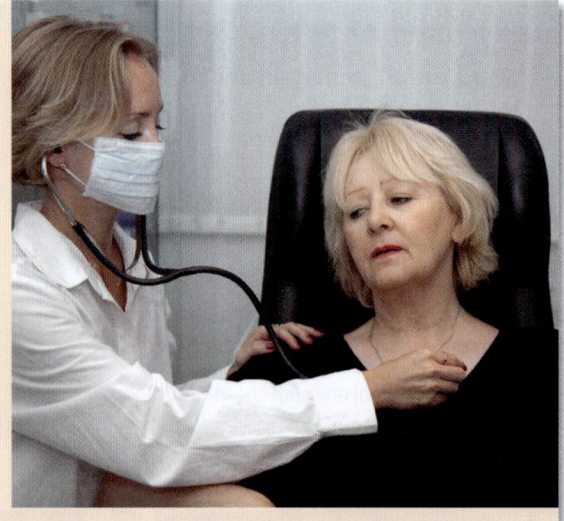

1 ☐ These centres provide a complete range of NHS dental services, including routine as well as urgent care. People do not need to register to see a dentist in an access centre and the centres are open at times when patients can get to them.

2 ☐ The first point of contact for many people when they develop a health problem is their local doctor, also known as a general practitioner (GP). These doctors usually form a small practice, or surgery, to serve a particular neighbourhood. GPs look after the health of people in their local community and deal with a whole range of health problems.

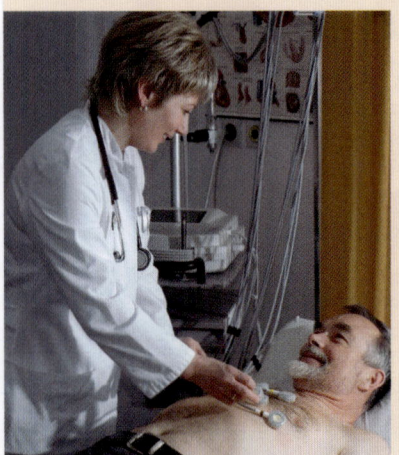

3 ☐ These centres offer fast access to health advice and treatment. They are open and available to anyone and provide:

- a seven days a week service, from early in the morning until late in the evening.
- assessment by an experienced NHS nurse.
- treatment for minor injuries and illnesses.
- advice on how to stay healthy.
- information on local services.

4 ☐ This is the gateway to health advice and information on the Internet. It includes an easy-to-use guide to treating common symptoms at home and links to thousands of sources of help and advice.

Health & fitness

Writing

ISE → See ISE file on page 88

6 Now write a descriptive essay (100-130 words) for a health magazine about the free healthcare services that are available in Britain and in your country. Say which are most useful for patients and why.

Phonology

■ **Intonation patterns of more complex question forms**

7a 🔊 Listen to the questions and draw arrows where the voice goes up and down.

0 What do you think about getting healthcare advice on the Internet?
1 Have you ever been to a hospital? If so, was it to visit someone or because you were ill?
2 When did you last visit your GP? What was wrong with you?
3 What are the opening times of your local surgery? What happens if you're ill when it's closed?
4 How often do you go to the dentist's? How do you feel about going?

b 🔊 Listen again and repeat the questions.

c Work with a partner. Ask and answer the questions in a).

d Are these statements true (T) or false (F), according to the text?

1 ☐ Dental access centres only provide a service for emergencies.
2 ☐ Dental access centres are only open during normal working hours, e.g. 9 a.m.-5 p.m.
3 ☐ A GP is another name for a local doctor.
4 ☐ GPs look after people in a specific area.
5 ☐ Anyone can go to an NHS walk-in centre.
6 ☐ You can see a doctor at an NHS walk-in centre.
7 ☐ At NHS walk-in centres, you can find out lots of information about health.
8 ☐ NHS Direct online gives advice to help people treat minor illnesses themselves.

71

exam EXPERT

Conversation
■ Health and fitness

9a Work with a partner and follow these instructions.

1. Make a list of the different areas of health and fitness the examiner may ask you about in the Conversation phase. Refer to exercises 1, 4 and 5 for help.

   E.g. keeping fit

2. Now prepare some questions for the examiner to ask about each of the areas on your list and think about how the candidate could answer the questions. Try and use some (G5)G6/ISE I language in your questions.

   What activities have you tried to keep fit? Well, I've played football and tried running. What must someone do to keep fit? They have to do regular exercise. Going to the gym is a good idea.

3. Prepare two questions that the candidate could ask the examiner about health and fitness.

b One of you is Student A, the other Student B. Student A read the examiner rolecard and Student B read the candidate rolecard. Follow the instructions.

c Now change roles and repeat stages 1-2.

Student A: Examiner

Stage 1 Have a conversation with the candidate (Student B) about health and fitness. Use the questions you prepared above. Answer the question/s that the candidate asks you.

Stage 2 Decide with Student B what went well in the conversation and what you could improve. Your teacher will also give you some ideas.

Don't forget, in the exam you can't do a topic on one of the Subject areas for conversation, so topics about Health and Fitness in general would not be a suitable choice for the actual exam (but a particular sport would be fine).

Student B: Candidate

Stage 1 Have a conversation with the examiner (Student A) about health and fitness. Remember to ask the examiner at least one question.

Stage 2 Decide with Student A what went well in the conversation and what you could improve. Your teacher will also give you some ideas.

Topic phase
■ Choosing a topic

10a Work with a partner. Make a list of 10 possible topics to talk about in the Topic phase.

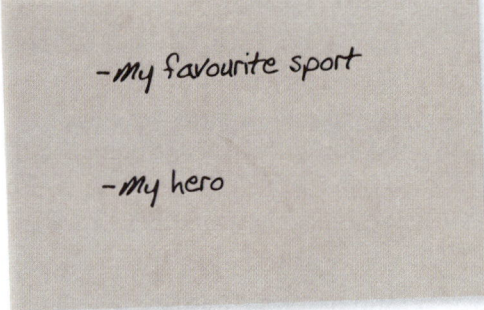
- my favourite sport
- my hero

b Compare your list with another pair. Add any of their topics that you haven't got on your list.

c Choose the topic from your list that you are most interested in.

exam EXPERT

d Ask your partner these questions.

1. What topic did you choose in c)?
2. Are you really interested in this topic?
3. Can you say something about this topic in your own language?
4. Do you know any vocabulary for this topic already in English?
5. Will you feel comfortable talking about this topic in English?
6. Do you want to know more about this topic?
7. Will you feel confident answering questions about this topic?
8. Is there enough to say about this topic to speak for five minutes?

e If you answered 'yes' to questions 2-8 in d), then it is a good subject for you to choose for practice, but make sure that in the exam your topic is not on one of the Subject areas for the Conversation phase. If not, look back at your list in b) and choose another one.

f With the topic you have chosen in c) or e), plan three things to say about it now. Ask your teacher for any vocabulary you need.

g Work with a partner. Take it in turns to present the three points you planned in f) about your topic. Ask your partner at least three questions about the points they make.

Writing

ISE → See ISE file on pages 89 and 91

11 Choose one of these questions.

An email

You have recently become very fit. Write an email (100-130 words) to a friend. You should:

- explain what you were doing wrong before you became fit
- say what you have done to reach this new level of fitness.

An article

A fast food restaurant has just opened in your area. Write an article (100-130 words) for a healthy eating organisation. You should:

- explain why the food at the restaurant is unhealthy
- say what health problems people might have if they eat a lot of fast food.

Examiner: What do you think is the best way to have a healthy lifestyle?
Candidate: Well, it's really important to have a healthy diet, for example, to eat five portions of fruit and vegetables a day and to eat fish regularly too. If you do some exercise two or three times a week, you can keep fit too.

Review Units 5-8

1 **Circle the correct option in the sentences (1–8).**

1. You can't go to the party in those clothes! You look really *smart/scruffy*!
2. Look at that jacket! It's so *cool/old-fashioned*! I love it, but it's too expensive!
3. Those trousers don't *suit/fit* you anymore – I think you've grown!
4. That dress really *suits/matches* you – it's exactly the same colour as your eyes.
5. My grandmother always tries to pay *by cheque/in cash*, but they don't accept them in lots of places nowadays.
6. I like going *on package holidays/backpacking* – I don't have to make any plans myself, it's all organised for me!
7. My brother always stays at *bed and breakfast places/youth hostels* when he's on holiday, because they're cheap.
8. My parents like staying in *hotels/self-catering accommodation* when we go away, so that they don't have to do any cooking!

2 **Complete the sentences with the correct form of the verb in brackets, the Past Continuous or Past Simple.**

1. I .... (*backpack*) in Turkey when I first .... (*meet*) my boyfriend.
2. It .... (*rain*), so we .... (*decide*) not to go for a walk.
3. I .... (*do*) my homework when they .... (*arrive*).
4. We .... (*shop*) for six hours, but .... (*not find*) the right dress for the wedding.
5. I .... (*get*) really fit last year – I .... (*exercise*) a lot and .... (*eat*) really well.

3 It's Sunday evening. Marina is talking on the phone to a friend about her plans for the next week. Look at her diary and write what she says about her plans for each day using the Present Continuous + future time reference.

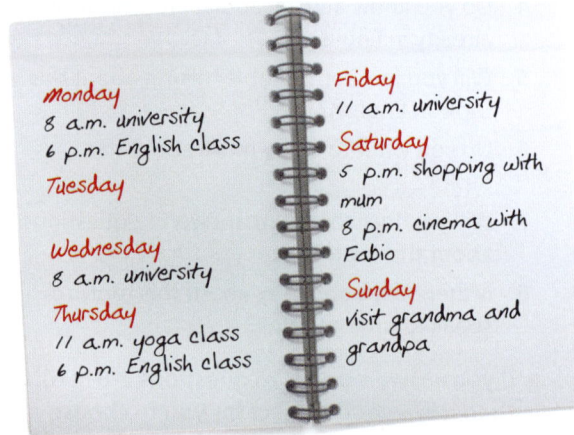

Monday
8 a.m. university
6 p.m. English class

Tuesday

Wednesday
8 a.m. university

Thursday
11 a.m. yoga class
6 p.m. English class

Friday
11 a.m. university

Saturday
5 p.m. shopping with mum
8 p.m. cinema with Fabio

Sunday
visit grandma and grandpa

4 **Complete the sentences (1–6) using *have to*, *must*, *don't have to*, *mustn't* and *might*.**

1. Emilio's parents give him a lot of freedom – he .... be home by any particular time the evenings.
2. Poor Lucy. She .... be home by 10 p.m., even on Saturdays!
3. If you fail an exam, you .... give up. You just .... work harder the next time!
4. You .... find learning another language hard when you first start.
5. You .... get depressed if you make mistakes – that's how you learn!
6. I .... wear a hat in the swimming pool and I hate it!

Review Units 5-8

5 Find words about healthcare people and places in Unit 8 to match the definitions (1-5).

1. The place where you go to see your local doctor. ....
2. The person who looks after you in hospital. ....
3. If you need new glasses, you go to see this person. ....
4. The person that you buy medicine from. ....
5. There are two words for this place where you buy medicine. ....

6 Match the two halves (1-6 and A-F) of the following conditional sentences.

1. If you go into town this afternoon,
2. If we don't hurry up,
3. You may lose some weight,
4. He'll fail his exams,
5. If you want to be healthy,
6. If you're having a good time,

A ☐ if he doesn't study harder.
B ☐ I may come with you.
C ☐ if you eat less fatty food.
D ☐ we'll miss the train!
E ☐ you need to drink at least two litres of water per day.
F ☐ we'll stay for longer.

7 Match candidates' questions from the Conversation phase (1-6) with the examiner's answers (A-F).

1. Are you interested in fashion?
2. Do you travel much?
3. In the UK, do you normally give tips?
4. Have you seen the new Harry Potter film?
5. When you travel, do you prefer to use cash or credit cards?
6. What do you do to keep fit?

A ☐ Not really, no, not now. But I was when I was younger.
B ☐ Yes, quite a lot, with my job. And then on holiday a couple of times a year.
C ☐ Yes, usually, unless you're really not happy with the service.
D ☐ Well, actually, I always take both with me, then I've always got a way of paying!
E ☐ Well, I go running about three times a week, and I do yoga whenever I can.
F ☐ Yes, I saw it last week. I thought it was great!

Grade 6 Self-evaluation

Write Y (yes) or N (needs more practice) for each statement.

1. ☐ I can talk about fashion.
2. ☐ I can talk about money.
3. ☐ I can talk about travel.
4. ☐ I can talk about learning a language.
5. ☐ I can talk about rules and regulation.
6. ☐ I can talk about health and fitness.
7. ☐ I can talk about future plans using the Present Continuous + future time expression.
8. ☐ I can use *have to*, *need to*, *must*, *don't have to*, *mustn't* and *might* accurately.
9. ☐ I can use the first conditional accurately.

1 Focus on the Topic phase for Grades 5 and 6 and ISE I

In the Topic phase you will talk about the topic that you have prepared. The examiner will ask you questions depending on what your topic is about. He/she will choose points from your Topic form and ask you about these in random order.

Typical examiner and candidate language at the start of this phase is:

Examiner: Hello, my name's Simon. What's your name?
Candidate: My name's Xavier Fernandez.

Examiner: Nice to meet you, Xavier. Can I have your Topic form, please?
Candidate: Yes, here you are.

2a Focus on the Conversation phase for Grades 5 and 6

The examiner will choose **two** of the **subject areas** for the grade (see **Overview**, pages 4-5) and will expect you to discuss these. You need to learn the vocabulary and prepare all six subject areas for the grade. The examples below show possible examiner and candidate language for each grade.

2b Focus on the Conversation phase for ISE I

The examiner will choose **one** of the **subject areas** for ISE I (see **Overview**, page 5) and will expect you to discuss it. You need to learn the vocabulary and prepare all six subject areas for the level. These are the same as those for Grade 6.

GRADE 5

Examiner: Do you celebrate a lot of festivals in your country?
Candidate: Yes, we celebrate many festivals, but I think the most important one is carnival, in February.

Examiner: Which means of transport do people in your city prefer?
Candidate: Well, they prefer the underground because it's the fastest way, but the bus is cheaper.

Examiner: Will you spend Christmas with your family this year?
Candidate: Yes, definitely. We always eat lunch with my aunt and uncle on 25th December.

Examiner: Have you seen any good films recently?
Candidate: Yes, I've seen the new Harry Potter film.

Examiner: Which do you prefer, hip hop or pop music?
Candidate: I prefer listening to hip hop. What about you, do you like pop music?
Examiner: Yes, I do, but I prefer classical music!

Examiner: Have you done anything special recently?
Candidate: Yes, I went to Bilbao two weeks ago, because my cousin lives there.

Trinity Takeaway

GRADE 6

Examiner: What were the tourists doing when the tour guide was speaking?
Candidate: Some were looking at the Eiffel Tower and others were taking photographs.

Examiner: Do you have to help your parents in the house?
Candidate: No, but if I don't, they don't give me any pocket money.

Examiner: If you go to the party on Saturday, what will you wear?
Candidate: I think I'll go shopping on Saturday to buy something new.

Examiner: What time does school start?
Candidate: Well, lessons start at 9 o'clock, but we have to be there at 8.50 for registration.

Examiner: Do you prefer playing sport or watching it?
Candidate: I prefer playing sport, but this weekend I'm watching Arsenal play against Liverpool.

Examiner: What is the best way to remember new vocabulary in English?
Candidate: If I write an example sentence using each word, it helps me to remember the vocabulary.

ISE file

Task 1 – Long Reading

1 Read the following text about train travel in Europe and answer the 15 questions below.

Are trains the way to travel across Europe?

Paragraph 1

For some people, the train has always been the best way to travel across Europe. You can watch the beautiful scenery go by while relaxing in your seat. You can talk to other passengers. You can sit comfortably and read a book instead of reading maps to get to your destination. You can also, most importantly, arrive directly in the city centre and not worry about car parking spaces or long journeys from the airport.

Paragraph 2

Of course, one of the best reasons to travel by train is that it's good for the planet. Trains are more environmentally friendly than planes or cars. While you watch the countryside from your train window, you can be confident that you are damaging it less by train than if you had travelled by car or plane. In Europe, some trains now have an upstairs and downstairs, very similar to London buses. This means that even more people can travel on the same train, so reducing further the impact of train travel on the environment.

Paragraph 3

However, keeping stations modern and train lines up to date is expensive. Many train services don't make enough money to cover costs. This means that railway companies often have to make difficult choices, like closing stations in villages and small towns or cutting night trains. They may also reduce services, making travelling across the continent by train more complicated for passengers.

Paragraph 4

With the rise of low-cost airlines in Europe, increasingly people are choosing to travel by plane, rather than train. These airlines fly to more cities than ever before, and journey times are much shorter than going by train. International flights are simple to book online and, if before it was expensive to fly, now it's becoming cheaper and cheaper. It's difficult for trains to compete with this.

Paragraph 5

It's not all bad news for European train travel, however. There are now high-speed train links between many European cities, e.g. Barcelona and Paris. From the customer service point of view, there are now websites which help passengers book long-distance train travel in a few simple clicks. Passengers today can also benefit from a wide range of special offers and rail passes offering discount prices on travel. Technological advances mean that battery-powered trains could be possible in the near future, so reducing further the impact of train travel on the environment. With these developments, taking the train could once again become the favourite way of getting around Europe.

ISE file

Questions 1-5 (one mark per question)

The text has five paragraphs (1-5). Choose the best title for each paragraph from A-F below and **write the letter (A-F) on the lines below**. There is one title you don't need.

1. Paragraph 1 ....
2. Paragraph 2 ....
3. Paragraph 3 ....
4. Paragraph 4 ....
5. Paragraph 5 ....

A The benefits of train travel for the environment
B Why people take planes instead of trains
C The benefits for passengers of travelling by train
D Train travel in the future
E Recent developments in European rail travel
F Cut backs in European rail services

Questions 6-10 (one mark per question)

Choose the five statements from A-H below that are TRUE according to the information given in the text. **Write the letters of the TRUE statements on the lines below (in any order)**.

6. ....
7. ....
8. ....
9. ....
10. ....

A There is a similarity between some European trains and London buses.
B Having to talk to other passengers is one of the disadvantages of train travel.
C Trains have lost passengers to planes because of price and speed.
D Reducing train services makes it easier for passengers to choose which train to take.
E Decisions about cuts to rail services are not easy for European railway companies.
F Trains that run on batteries operate between Barcelona and Paris.
G Train travel could go back to being the way people prefer to travel in Europe.
H The text mentions that it is easier nowadays to book tickets online for both trains and plane.

Questions 11-15 (one mark per question)

Complete sentences 11-15 with a word, phrase or number from the text (maximum three words). **Write the word, phrase or number on the lines below**.

11. One of the best things about trains is that they arrive right in the .... not a long way outside it like planes do.
12. An advantage of trains is that they're more .... than planes, i.e. they don't damage the environment so much.
13. It's expensive for train companies to keep train lines modern and ....
14. .... airlines have made air travel in Europe very cheap.
15. There are .... prices available on European rail tickets.

ISE file

Task 2 – Multi-text reading (1)

As part of your studies you are going to read about sleep. In this section there are four short texts for you to read and some questions for you to answer.

Questions 16-20 (one mark per question)

Read questions 16-20 first and then read texts A, B, C and D below the questions.

As you read each text, decide which text each question refers to. **Choose one letter – A, B, C or D – and write it on the lines below**. You can use any letter more than once.

Which text

16. complains about how teenagers don't get the chance to sleep late? ....
17. explains how students might get better exam grades if they sleep more? ....
18. shows how little sleep teenagers get? ....
19. describes an experiment happening in schools at the moment? ....
20. criticises the idea of teenagers starting school later in the morning? ....

Text A

Let teenagers sleep in the morning

Researchers at Oxford University have recently started a new experiment in a large number of schools around the UK. From 2014-2018, thousands of 15 and 16 year olds will start school at 10.00 instead of 8.30 or 9.00. The researchers want to prove that a later school start leads to better marks in exams. We have known for a long time that the average teenager needs a minimum of nine hours sleep a night. However, very few get this much sleep during the week. This is because teenagers are biologically programmed to fall asleep later at night and wake up later the next morning. But lessons start early. Scientists believe that allowing teenagers to sleep more would give positive results. These include more students attending school and fewer students falling asleep at their desks. And, of course, better exam results.

Text B

Dear Sir or Madam,

I read your article on teenagers and sleep with interest. However, I think these scientists are worrying only about school results and not about other things which are equally important. I have a 16-year-old son who loves sports. Football training is after school, but if school starts and finishes later, when will he have time to practise? This would be the same for any other after-school activity – music, sports, dance etc. My son also works in a café on a Friday afternoon. The job gives him independence and teaches him the value of hard work. Other parents have the same opinion as I do. How could he do this if he finishes school at 5pm? Teenagers need to have interests out of school, but this can only happen if they finish early enough to follow them.

Yours faithfully,
Lucy Brown

Text C

To all those teenagers out there... Do you think you get enough sleep?

 Annie: How can I get enough sleep when I have so much homework? Like my friends, I study until midnight every evening.

 Hassan: The teachers always say I look tired but I can't help it. Lessons start so early.

Mary: I need to sleep more at the weekends but I can't. My mum is always telling me to tidy my room.

 Nimal: @Hassan My swimming instructor wants me in the pool before school. I'd love to start lessons after 9.00.

 Josh: The problem is my computer. I always spend so long seeing what my friends are doing before I go to bed that I go to sleep very late.

 Brad: @Mary, I understand. My grandparents come for lunch every Sunday and I always have to get up early to help clean the house before they arrive!

Vanessa: @Josh My friends send me messages during the night and wake me up. But I don't want to switch off the phone in case I miss something.

Text D

Teenage boys and girls: hours of sleep per night

Girls

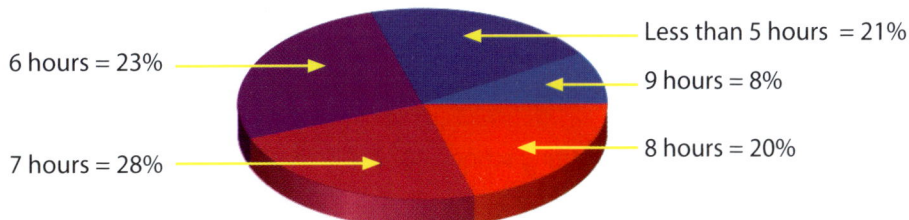

6 hours = 23%
7 hours = 28%
Less than 5 hours = 21%
9 hours = 8%
8 hours = 20%

Boys

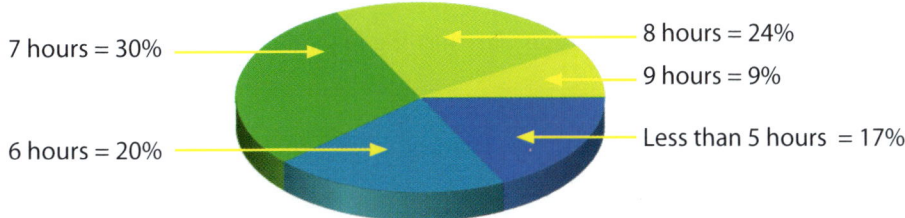

7 hours = 30%
6 hours = 20%
8 hours = 24%
9 hours = 9%
Less than 5 hours = 17%

ISE file

Questions 21-25 (one mark per question)

Choose the five statements from A-H below that are **TRUE** according to the information given in the texts above. **Write the letters of the TRUE statements on the lines below (in any order)**.

21. ....
22. ....
23. ....
24. ....
25. ....

A Not all schools in the UK will start classes at 10.00.

B More boys than girls get the full of amount of sleep they need per night.

C Some parents think it's good for their children to work after school.

D Experts say teenagers must get at least 9 hours sleep a night to do well at sports.

E Two teenagers talk about doing housework at the weekend.

F With the new school timetable, teenagers will have time to do sports activities during the school day.

G One teenager talks about going to bed late because they are doing homework on their computer.

H Most girls sleep 7 hours per night.

Questions 26-30 (One mark per question)

The summary notes below contain information on the texts on pages 80 and 81. **Find a word or phrase (maximum three words) from texts A- D to complete the missing information in gaps 26-30**.

Write your answers on the lines below.

Summary notes

Teenage sleep patterns

Most teenagers sleep less than they need

Teenagers are (**26**) .... to go to bed and get up later than adults

Teenagers should sleep a minimum of 9 hours per night

Expert ideas

Experts from Oxford University have started an (**27**) .... with 15 and 16 year olds

Some scientists want to see if starting school (**28**) .... will help teenagers at school

Some teenagers fall asleep in class

People's opinions

Some teenagers do not get enough hours of sleep because of the (**29**) .... they have to do.

Other teenagers spend time chatting with their friends and don't go to bed early enough

Some parents think that (**30**) .... are not the only important things in a teenager's life

Teenagers need to have time to do different things after school

Task 3 – Reading and Writing

You are doing a project on sleep and you need to write a short essay for your teacher (100-130 words) about teenagers and sleep.

Use the information you read in Task 2 (pages 80 to 82) to:
- describe the sleeping habits of an average teenager
- explain why some schools are trying to change the school programme
- say if these changes are popular with everyone.

You should plan your essay **before** you start writing. Think about what you want to say and make some notes to help you in this box:

Planning notes
....
....
....
....
....
....
....
....
....
....

(No marks are given for these planning notes)

Now write your essay of 100-130 words. Try to use your own words as far as possible – don't just copy sentences from the reading texts.

Task 2 – Multi-text reading (2)

As part of your studies you are going to read about changes in the music industry. In this section there are four short texts for you to read and some questions for you to answer.

Questions 16-20 (one mark per question)

Read questions 16-20 first and then read texts A, B, C and D below the questions.

As you read each text, decide which text each question refers to. **Choose one letter – A, B, C or D – and write it on the lines below**. You can use any letter more than once.

Which text
16. explains why a musician has decided to remove his music from streaming sites?
   ....
17. shows how streaming in music has become much more important in North America?
   ....
18. describes how the music industry is completely different now from in the past? ....
19. gives details on how little a musician is paid by on-line streaming sites? ....
20. makes positive comments about digital music? ....

ISE file

Text A

Changes in the music world

The music industry has changed because of the Internet and digital music. How we discover, listen to and buy our music has changed forever. We no longer have to go into a store and buy music, but we can organise it all from our computer or mobile phone. Sales of CDs have fallen. Even downloading music seems to be less popular than before. Nowadays, more and more people listen to a wide variety of music using streaming sites such as Pandora or Spotify. These kinds of sites have made more music than ever before available to more people all over the world – and at a cheaper price. But the growing popularity of digital music has not been so popular with record companies or musicians, who now make less money from the music.

Text B

From: Nick Rock
Sent: 20 September 2015
To: editor@musicmag.co.uk
Subject: Why I'm taking my music off streaming services

Dear Editor,
From today, my music will no longer be available on-line via streaming websites. These sites give my music away for free or at a very low cost. I feel that my music has a value and that people should pay to listen to what I have created. These sites pay the music companies a very small amount. The companies then give the musician very little money each time a song is played.
Fans will still be able to buy and download my albums and, of course, find them in the shops. And I hope they will understand why I have done this.
Yours,
Nick

Text C

Music companies say that the Internet is killing music. Do you think this is true?

 Darius: Music is far too expensive. Perhaps iTunes aren't selling as many songs as before, but musicians are still making lots more money than other people in the country.

 Maggie: I've discovered so much new music through sites like Pandora. It's great.

 Lea: I have all my music on my phone and can listen to it everywhere. You can't do that with CDs.

 Mark: I still spend money on music. Instead of buying one CD, I download individual songs from lots of groups.

 Darius: @Maggie I know. It's great. I've bought lots of songs that I first heard on Pandora.

 Alana: @Maggie Streaming is keeping music alive. You discover a new band. You go to see them in concert. More bands should realise this is how to make money nowadays.

ISE file

 Maggie: @Alana Exactly. Even if the price of tickets has gone up I still prefer to spend my money on concerts. Often the musician earns more through singing live than through loads of downloads and streaming!

Text D

Number of songs streamed in the USA

2013 – 106 billion songs streamed
2014 – 164 billion songs streamed

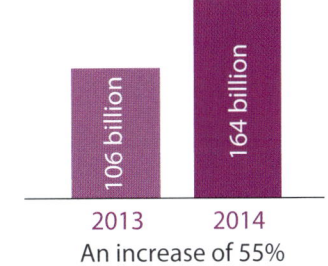
An increase of 55%

Percentage of streaming of total music sales in the USA

2007 – 3%
2010 – 7%
2013 – 21%

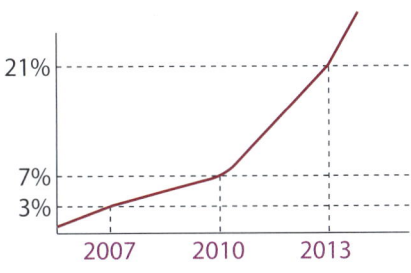

Questions 21-25 (one mark per question)

Choose the five statements from A-H below that are **TRUE** according to the information given in the texts above. **Write the letters of the TRUE statements on the lines below (in any order).**

21. ....
22. ....
23. ....
24. ....
25. ....

A People say that they listen to music through streaming sites instead of going to see bands playing live concerts.
B Between 2013 and 2014 the number of songs streamed increased by more than half.
C Streaming has given music a more international audience.
D The online streaming sites pay the musicians directly.
E iTunes sales are decreasing.
F It's possible for musicians to stop streaming sites playing their music.
G Downloading music is just as popular as listening to music via streaming.
H Musicians can often make more money through concerts than downloads and streaming.

Questions 26-30 (One mark per question)

The summary notes below contain information on the texts on pages 84 and 85. **Find a word or phrase (maximum three words) from texts A-D to complete the missing information in gaps 26-30.**

ISE file

Write your answers on the lines below.

Summary notes

Changes in the music industry
Music now available via the Internet
People can download music from places such as iTunes
Sales through streaming increased to (**26**) .... % of total music sales in 2013
More music is available to people in different countries

Advantages for music fans
Streaming music is cheaper than (**27**) .... or buying CDs
You can listen to a choice of music on sites like Pandora or Spotify
You can discover new bands on these sites and then go and listen to them in (**28**) ....

Disadvantages for the music industry
Musicians receive (**29**) .... when a site plays one of their songs
Some musicians feel that their music has no (**30**) .... if it's given away for free
Music companies now make less money

Task 3 – Reading and Writing

You are doing a project on digital music and you need to write an essay (100-130 words) for your teacher about changes in the music industry.

Use the information you read in Task 2 (pages 83 to 86) to:
- describe how the music industry has changed
- say why these changes have not been good for people in the music industry
- explain how these changes have had a positive effect.

You should plan your essay **before** you start writing. Think about what you want to say and make some notes to help you in this box:

Planning notes
....
....
....
....
....
....
....
....
....

(No marks are given for these planning notes)

Now write your essay of 100-130 words. Try to use your own words as far as possible – don't just copy sentences from the reading texts.

ISE file

Task 4 – Extended Writing: a discursive essay

1 Work with a partner. Discuss your ideas on team sports and individual sports, saying which you think is better. Give your reasons.

2 Read the task and the essay. Are any ideas from your discussion in 1 mentioned?

Write an essay (100-130 words) with the title 'Team sports versus individual sports'. You should:
- explain what you think about these types of sport
- say which type of sport you prefer.

1 In this essay I will discuss my ideas on two types of sport. These are team sports, like basketball, and individual sports like running.

2 Firstly, in team sports, you have to work together with other people. If you don't do this, you might lose the match. Secondly, I think it is also enjoyable to do sport with your friends.

3 On the other hand, in my opinion, individual sports are tougher. They are good for you because you are responsible for your own success. You can't rely on anyone else. These sports are not so much fun because you train and compete on your own.

4 In general, it is good for young people to do any kind of sport. Personally, I prefer team sports because of the friendships you make and because you work with other people to win.

3 Read the essay again. Match the paragraphs (1-4) with their functions (a-d).

a ☐ Concluding the argument. c ☐ Introducing the topic.
b ☐ Writing about the first part of the task. d ☐ Writing about the second part of the task

4 Complete the guidelines about writing discursive essays with a word from the box.

> introduction   link   contraction   neutral   paragraphs

- Organise it into ¹......................... : 1) introduction, 2) the first part of the task, 3) the second part of the task, 4) conclusion.
- Explain in the ²......................... what you are going to write about in the essay, e.g. *In this essay I will discuss my ideas on two types of sport.*
- Use words and expressions to introduce and ³......................... the points you make, e.g. *In my opinion,..., On the one hand..., On the other hand..., A positive point is..., A negative point is..., Firstly, Secondly..., ...because ...*
- The style of language should generally be formal, but the following more ⁴......................... features can be used: when talking about people in general, use *you*, e.g. **you** *might lose the match...,* *They are good for* **you** *because ...,* use the ⁵......................... **don't** instead of *do not* and **can't** instead of *cannot*.

5 Plan an essay for the following task. Think about what points to include and make notes.

Write an essay (100-130 words) for your school website with the title 'School uniform – a good idea?' You should:
- explain what the rules are about clothes for school in your country
- give your own opinion about school uniforms.

6 Write your essay. Use your notes from Ex. 5 and follow the guidelines about writing essays in Ex. 4.

7 Check your essay. Have you included enough relevant points? Have you organised it correctly? Have you followed the guidelines from Ex. 4?

ISE file

Task 4 – Extended Writing: a descriptive essay

1 Work with a partner. Make a list of what you think makes a town or city a good place to live.

2 Read the task and the essay in response to it. Are any of the things from your list in Exercise 1 mentioned?

Your class is doing a project on towns and cities. Your teacher has asked you to write an esssay (100-130 words) with the title 'A good place to live'. You should:
- explain what makes a town or a city a good place to live
- give your opinion on what is the most important of these ideas.

A good place to live

What makes a town or city a good place to live is just a matter of personal opinion, but there are some ideas that most people probably agree on.

First of all, a place needs a fast and efficient public transport system, so that people can move around the city easily. Something else that's important is to have enough places to buy reasonably-priced food and other products, so that people don't have to go to out-of-town shopping centres. Having plenty of sports and entertainment facilities so that people have things to do in their free time is also important. Finally, public parks help make a city a nice place to live, providing green spaces for people to exercise and relax in.

All of the above ideas are important, but one that's essential for me is that a town or city is safe, because cities with a high crime rate can be difficult places to live.

3 Read the essay again and complete the guidelines about writing a descriptive essay with words and phrases from the box.

> adjectives   concluding   connecting   ideas   title

- Give the essay a ¹........................ to make it clear what it's about, e.g. *A good place to live*.
- Structure the essay as follows: an introduction, the main body (one or two paragraphs) and a ²........................ paragraph. Organise your ³........................ logically within these paragraphs.
- Use ⁴........................ words and phrases for sequencing, e.g. *First of all, Finally*, and for adding comments on the same topic, e.g. *Something else that's important is...*, *(Sports and entertainment facilities) is/are also important*.
- Use varied ⁵........................ and adverbs to make the description interesting to read, e.g. *efficient, reasonably-priced, essential*.

4 Plan an essay for the following task. Think about what points to include and make notes.

Your class is doing a project on towns and cities. Your teacher has asked you to write an essay (100-130 words) with the title 'A good town or city for a holiday'. You should:
- say what a town or city needs to be good for a holiday
- describe a town or city you think is a good place for a holiday.

5 Write your essay. Use your notes from Exercise 4 and follow the guidelines about writing a descriptive essay from Exercise 3.

6 Check your essay. Have you included enough relevant points? Have you organised it correctly? Have you followed the guidelines from Exercise 3?

ISE file

Task 4 – Extended Writing: an article

1 Work with a partner. Discuss what you think can be causes of stress for people today, and what the symptoms of stress can be.

2 Read the task and the email in response to it. Are any of the things that you discussed in Exercise 1 mentioned?

Many people today complain that they suffer from stress. Write an article (100-130 words) for the health section of a student magazine. You should:
• explain why people suffer from stress these days
• describe what people have to do to reduce stress.

Stressed out?

'I'm so stressed!' How often do you hear people saying that or have you said it yourself? But is it really true? And what can you do about it?

Being unhappy in a relationship, feeling under pressure at school or work or being seriously worried about money or the future can all be causes of real stress. If you feel tired a lot, or don't feel like eating or regularly eat too much, or have problems concentrating on studying or work, or if you're finding it difficult to make decisions, then you may really be stressed.

What do you have to do to reduce stress? You mustn't have drinks with caffeine, like coffee or cola, and you must eat well – no junk food! Do exercise because you'll feel better. Finally, if you talk about your problems, this will really help.

3 Read the article again. Complete the guidelines about writing articles with a word from the box.

> *examples   paragraphs   question   readers   title   writer*

- Include a ¹.......................... .
- Start the article with an interesting statement or ².......................... that attracts the reader's attention, e.g. I'm so stressed!
- Organise the article into ³..........................: introduction, main body and conclusion.
- Language style – informal, neutral or formal – should be appropriate for the ⁴.........................., e.g. informal to neutral for a student magazine.
- Articles will often include the ⁵..........................'s opinion.
- We often give ⁶.......................... in articles, e.g. like coffee or cola, no junk food!

4 Plan an article for the following task. Think about what points to include and make notes.

Some young people are not very fit these days. Write an article (100-130 words) about young people's fitness for a health magazine. You should:
• say why you think some young people are not very fit
• explain what they have to do to become fitter.

5 Write your article. Use your notes from Exercise 4 and follow the guidelines about writing articles from Exercise 3.

6 Check your article. Have you included enough relevant points? Have you organised it correctly? Have you followed the guidelines from Exercise 3?

ISE file

Task 4 – Extended Writing: informal emails and letters

1. Work with a partner. Imagine that you are going on a trip together around the world for six months. Make a list of the places that you would like to visit.

2. Read the task and the email in response to it. Are any of the places from your list in Exercise 1 mentioned?

   You are planning to spend six months travelling around the world. Write an email (100-130 words) to a friend. You should:
   - *explain which countries you plan to visit*
   - *say what you will see on your trip.*

   > To: lucy@dundee.co.uk
   > Subject: News!
   >
   > Hi Lucy,
   > How are you?
   > I've got some exciting news to tell you. I'm going on a trip around the world for six months with my friend Clara! We're flying to New York at the beginning of July and we're spending a week there sightseeing. We'll see all the famous places. Then we're getting the train to Washington because Clara really wants to see the White House. After that, we're flying down to Mexico City and planning to spend two months travelling around Latin America – the Amazon River is the main thing that we'll see there. I'm so excited. We're not sure where we're going to go after that, but probably somewhere in Asia. We've got round-the-world plane tickets, so we can decide later. Pretty cool, don't you think?! Why don't you come with us? ☺ Let me know ASAP!
   > Speak soon,
   > Rosa x

3. Complete the guidelines about writing informal emails and letters with *do* or *don't*.

   - ¹……………… use informal language, e.g. *I've got, Pretty cool,* not formal language.
   - ²……………… use contractions, not full forms, e.g. *I'm,* not *I am,* and *we're,* not *we are.*
   - ³……………… use correct spelling and punctuation. ⁴……………… use text message spelling, e.g. *C* for *see, R* for *are,* but ⁵……………… use standard abbreviations such as *asap* (as soon as possible) and emoticons, e.g. ☺
   - ⁶……………… include an appropriate opening, e.g. *Hi Lucy,* and ending, e.g. *Take care, See you soon, Speak soon, Bye for now, Love* (to a partner, family member of close friend), or *All the best,* to someone you don't know very well.
   - ⁷……………… add an 'x' after your name at the end to represent a kiss, but ⁸……………… add this if you don't know the person you're writing to very well!

4. Plan an informal email for the following task. Think about what points to include and make notes.

   You have won a 6-week holiday for you and a friend in the USA. Write an email (100-130 words) to your friend. You should:
   - *explain which places you want to visit on the holiday*
   - *say why you think your friend will enjoy the holiday.*

5. Write your email. Use your notes from Exercise 4 and follow the guidelines about writing informal emails from Exercise 3.

6. Check your email. Have you included enough relevant points? Have you organised it correctly? Have you followed the guidelines from Exercise 3?

ISE file

Task 4 – Extended Writing: formal emails and letters

1. Work with a partner. You have decided to go on an English language course in the UK this summer. Make a list of the things you would want to know about a course and a school before registering.

2. Read the task and the response to it. Which of the things in your list in in Exercise 1 are mentioned?

   You have seen an advert for English language courses at a school in London and you are interested in going there to do a course. Write a letter (100-130 words) to the principal of the college. You should:
   * *explain why you want to do the course*
   * *ask for further information about the course.*

   > Calle Serrano 18, 3ºB
   > Los Molinos
   > 287422
   > Madrid
   >
   > The Principal
   > London School of English
   > 12 Queen Street
   > London
   >
   > 19 April 2015
   >
   > Dear Sir/Madam,
   > I am interested in attending an English language course at your school and would like some information about the courses.
   > In my English classes here in Spain, we focus on learning grammar and vocabulary, and do not practise speaking and listening very much. That is why I am looking for a course that will help me improve my speaking and listening skills. Could you confirm that a course at your school would help me to do this?
   > I am able to attend a course in the summer. Could you let me know the dates of your courses in July and August? I would also like information about the price of the courses and details of places where I can stay.
   > I look forward to hearing from you.
   > Yours faithfully,
   > Esther García Jiménez

3. Read the letter again. Complete the guidelines about writing formal letters with a word from the box.

   > closing   contractions   date   emails   end   recipient   sender   start

   * The [1]................'s address goes on the top right-hand side, the [2]................'s address on the top left-hand side and the [3]................ below the sender's address.
   * If we [4]................ the letter with *Dear Sir/Madam*, we [5]................ it with *Yours faithfully*. If we start it with *Dear Mr Brown/Mrs Smith*, we end it with *Yours sincerely*. In formal [6]................, we would usually know the name of the person we're writing to and would end the email with *Regards* or *Best wishes*.
   * We can use *I look forward to hearing from you* as a way of [7]................ a letter or email.
   * We use neutral to formal language, e.g. *that is why* instead of *so*; *I am able to* instead of *I can*, *I would like you to* instead of *Can you...* This includes not using [8]................, e.g. *I am interested*, not *I'm interested*, and *I would like*, not *I'd like*.

ISE file

4 Plan a formal letter for the following task. Think about what points to include and make notes.

You have seen an advert for water sports (sailing, windsurfing, diving, etc.) activity holidays in the UK and you are interested in going to do one. Write a letter (100-130 words) to the company. You should:
• *explain why you want to go on one of their holidays*
• *ask for more information about this holiday.*

5 Write your letter. Use your notes from Exercise 4 and follow the guidelines about writing formal letters from Exercise 3.

6 Check your letter. Have you included enough relevant points? Have you organised it correctly? Have you followed the guidelines from Exercise 3?

Task 4 – Extended Writing: a review

1 Work with a partner. Discuss what you like and don't like about shopping centres. Then make a list of what you think would be the most important features of a shopping centre for young people.

2 Read the task and the review in response to it. Are any of the things that you discussed in Exercise 1 mentioned?

A new shopping centre has just opened in your town. Write a review (100-130 words) of the shopping centre for your school's online magazine. You should:
• *explain why young people will enjoy going there*
• *say if you think the students at your school will like it.*

> **Tilbury Super Centre**
>
> The new Tilbury Super Centre is open every day of the week.
>
> There are lots of great things for young people to do there. The clothes shops are great because they have all the latest fashions. There is also a sports shop. It is rather expensive, though. The best thing for many young people will be the enormous video games store.
>
> After shopping, there is the opportunity to go to a café or fast food restaurant. Young people will like the wide choice of food, from burgers to healthy salads.
>
> I think you'll all enjoy going there at the weekend for shopping. You'll love the variety of clothes and the prices are reasonable, too. You'll have a lot of fun with your friends. See you on Saturday?

3 Read the review again. Complete the guidelines about writing reviews with a word from the box.

| finish   go on   bad   three   start   title |

- Include a ¹......................., e.g. *Tilbury Super Centre*.
- Organise the review into ²....................... or four paragraphs.
- ³....................... by giving basic factual information, e.g. *The new Tilbury Super Centre is open every day of the week*.
- ⁴....................... to talk about good points – and mention ⁵....................... points where relevant, *It is rather expensive, though*. (Make sure you read the question – if it only asks for good points, you don't need to mention the negative points.)
- ⁶....................... with your opinion, saying if you think the reader will like it, e.g. *I think you'll enjoy going there...*

ISE file

4 Plan a review for the following task. Think about what points to include and make notes.

You recently went to a music festival. Write a review (100-130 words) for a music magazine. You should:
- *give your opinion of the festival*
- *say what you preferred about the festival.*

5 Write your review. Use your notes from Exercise 4 and follow the guidelines about writing reviews from Exercise 3.

Independent Listening – Task 1

1 You're going to listen to a short talk about the blue whale. Before you listen, work with a partner and make a list of any facts that you know about whales.

- very big
- mammals

2 🔊 Listen to the talk. As you listen, make notes about the facts that are mentioned.

3 🔊 Listen to the talk again. As you listen, check your notes and add to them as necessary.

4 Work with a partner. Take it in turns to ask the questions below about blue whales and to answer in one or two words using your notes from Exercises 2 and 3.

1. How long can an adult blue whale be?
2. The heaviest blue whale is the same weight as how many men?
3. What animal is the same weight as a blue whale's tongue?
4. How long do blue whales stay with their mothers?
5. How long is a baby whale when it is born?
6. How many miles away can you hear a blue whale's call?

5 Complete the guidelines about Independent Listening Task 1 with a word from the box.

> ask   concentrate   listen   make   prepare   refer (x2)   think

- When the examiner tells you what the talk is about, quickly **1**.................... what you know about the topic and any vocabulary in English connected with it. You won't have very much time to do this, but it will help **2**.................... you for what you're going to hear.
- You can **3**.................... the examiner for repetition or clarification of the instructions.
- You **4**.................... to the talk twice.
- The examiner will give you a Listening Exam Form and you can **5**.................... notes while the talk is playing. This is optional, but it's a good idea to do it! Don't worry about spelling when you're writing the notes – **6**.................... on what you're listening to, not what you're writing. Your notes aren't marked, they're just for you to **7**.................... to.
- After you've listened to the talk twice, the examiner will ask you six questions about it. You can **8**.................... to your notes when you answer.

93

ISE file

Independent Listening – Task 2

1. 🔊 Listen to a short podcast about a topic. After the talk, be prepared to say what the topic is.

2. 🔊 Listen to the podcast again. As you listen, make notes on facts that are mentioned about the topic from Exercise 1.

3. Work with a partner. Compare your facts from Exercise 2. Check that you have at least six.

4. Work alone. Write four extra questions about the podcast, to get more information about the facts from Exercises 2 and 3.

   What example is given in the podcast of two countries that have different forms of sign language?

   1 ....
   2 ....
   3 ....
   4 ....

5. With your partner from Exercise 3, ask and answer your extra questions about the podcast.

6. Complete the guidelines about Independent Listening Task 2 with a word from the box.

   facts   instructions   notes   questions   reference   six   topic   twice

   - The examiner doesn't tell you what the [1].................. of the listening task is – you have to listen to the podcast/talk, etc. and then tell the examiner what it is about.
   - You can ask for repetition or clarification of the [2].................. .
   - You listen [3].................. .
   - Before you listen the second time, the examiner will tell you that, after you have listened, you have to tell her [4].................. pieces of information about what you have heard.
   - As for Task 1, you can write [5].................. on the Listening Exam Form while you're listening. Again, this is optional, but it's a good idea to do it! Remember that your notes aren't marked, they're just for your [6].................. .
   - There will be more than six [7].................. in the podcast/talk. You have to tell the examiner six facts, but the examiner will ask you four extra questions about the podcast/talk, so you need to try and note down ten facts.
   - After you have told the examiner the six facts, she will ask you four extra [8].................. about these facts.

Extra material Appendix

Unit 3, page 26, exercise 3a

Film quiz answers:

1 B **2** A **3** B **4** C **5** C **6** B **7** C **8** A

Unit 5, page 44, exercise 5b

The following graphs show the percentage of income that people in different countries spend on four different things: housing, food & drink, health and education.

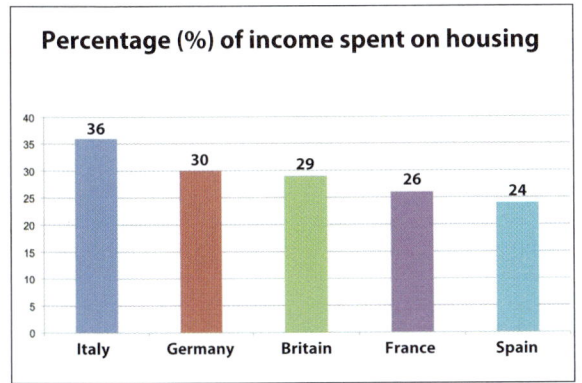
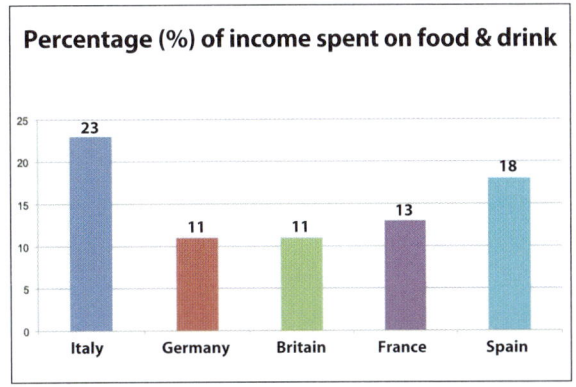
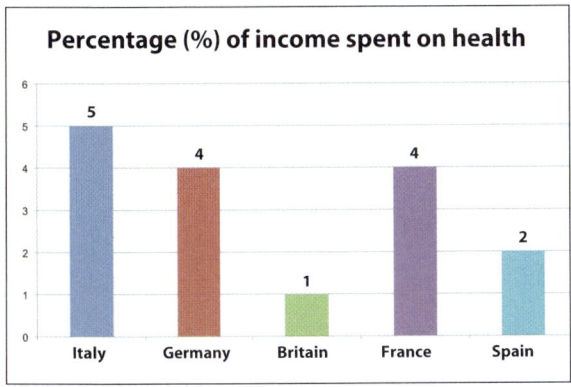
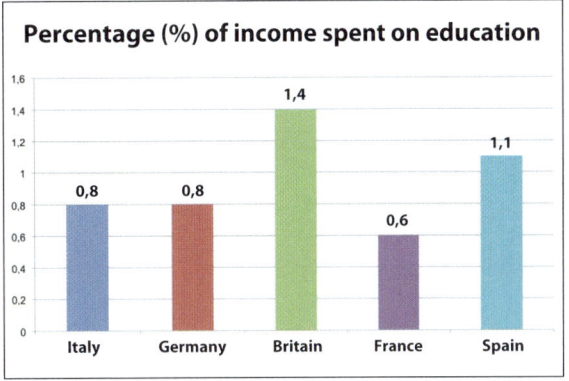

Unit 7, page 62, exercise 8b

1 Miami, USA **2** Singapore **3** Britain **4** Britain **5** France **6** Florida, USA **7** Vermont, USA **8** Britain **9** Athens, Greece **10** Arkansas, USA **11** Britain

95